# THE REVELATION
## OF DANIEL CHAPTERS 11-12

THE TIME OF THE END AND BEYOND

EDWARD D. ANDREWS

# THE REVELATION OF DANIEL CHAPTERS 11-12

## The Time of the End and Beyond

Edward D. Andrews

First Edition

Christian Publishing House

Cambridge, Ohio

*THE REVELATION OF DANIEL CHAPTERS 11-12: The Time of the End and Beyond* by Edward D. Andrews

ISBN-13: **978-1-949586-62-6**

**ISBN-10: 1-949586-62-6**

# Table of Contents

## Preface

In **Daniel Chapter 11**, we find two kings in opposition, fighting one conflict after another for power and dominion. As the decades go by, one will rise up while the other will fall, then the other accumulates domination. One king will be at the pinnacle of his rulership, while the other will be subservient. Then, out of nowhere, periods of peace. Suddenly, they emerge to battle once more. These kings are known as the kings of the North and the South. Over time, they change. The end is an event yet seen, far removed by millenniums from the initial kings. **Daniel chapter 12** delves into a question Jesus asked, "when the Son of Man comes, will he find faith on earth?" (Lu 18:8) The close of Daniel deals with the identity of the true worshipers in the time of the end. Furthermore, discover **when the great tribulation starts and how many years, months, and days it will last**. Andrews also offers three additional appendices to better understand Daniel and the end times. APPENDIX A What Does the Bible Really Say About the Millennium? APPENDIX B Authorship of Daniel Defended APPENDIX C Identifying the Antichrist.

# CHAPTER 1 The Kings of the South and the North - Daniel 11:1-9 (530 - 226 B.C.E.)

**Daniel 8:17, 19, 26** Updated American Standard Version (UASV)

17 So he came near where I stood. And when he came, I was frightened and fell on my face; but he said to me, "Understand, O son of man, that **the vision is for the time of the end.**" 19 And he said, "Look, I am making known to you what will happen in **the period of the wrath**, for it refers to **the appointed time of the end.** 26 The vision of the evenings and the mornings that has been told is true,[1] but **seal up the vision,**[2] for it refers to **many days from now.**"[3]

"The period of the wrath," has "the basic idea [of] experiencing or expressing intense anger. The word is parallel to *qāṣap*, except that its expression takes a more specific form, especially of denunciation."[4]

**Daniel 12:4, 9, 13** Updated American standard Version (UASV)

4 But as for you, O Daniel, **conceal these words** and **seal up the book** **until the time of the end**; many shall run to and fro,[5] and **knowledge will increase.**" 9 He said, "Go your way, Daniel, for the words are **shut up** and **sealed until the time of the end.** 13 But go your way till the end; and you shall rest and shall stand in your allotted place at **the end of the days.**"

The "time of wrath," connects it to "time of the end," and says: "It refers certainly to God's time of judgment on Israel at the time of Antiochus Epiphanes; but it refers also to God's future time of judgment during the great tribulation, in the last half of which the little horn of Daniel's first vision will bring even worse affliction" (Wood, Daniel, p. 106).

Campbell adds:

> It should also be noted that the expression "time of the end" occurs in Daniel 12:4 where it clearly means the time approaching Christ's Second Coming. The conclusion, then, is that we are to see

---

[1] Lit *truth*; Heb., *'emet*

[2] I.e., keep the vision secret; Heb., *satar*

[3] Lit *for to days many*; I.e., to the distant future

[4] Leon J. Wood, "568 זעם," ed. R. Laird Harris, Gleason L. Archer Jr., and Bruce K. Waltke, *Theological Wordbook of the Old Testament* (Chicago: Moody Press, 1999), 247.

[5] I.e. examine the book thoroughly

> an Antiochus Epiphanes a dread picture and symbol of Antichrist to come in the end time, or Tribulation" (Campbell, 126).

Kelly, West, Seiss, Pentecost, and Walvoord all support this dual reference approach to our passage. Walvoord says, "The entire chapter is historically filled in Antiochus, but to varying degrees foreshadowing typically the future world ruler who would dominate the situation at the end of the times of the Gentiles (Walvoord, Daniel, p. 196).

Archer, though hesitant, throws his considerable weight with this position as well:

> This interpretation has much to commend it, for Daniel makes clear through the assignment of the symbol of the "little horn" both to Antiochus of Kingdom III and to Antichrist of the latter-day phase of Kingdom IV that they bear to each other the relationship of type-antitype. Insofar as Epiphanes prefigured the determined effort to be made by the Beast to destroy the biblical faith, that prophecy that described the career of Antiochus also pertained to "the time of the end." Every type has great relevance for its antitype. But the future dealings of Antichrist can only be conjectured or surmised. Therefore, our discussion will be confined to the established deeds of Antiochus Epiphanes (Archer, p. 106).[6]

Some Bible scholars rightly understand these references to end times, as an increased understanding of the prophecies in the book of Daniel at that times. "Understandably **Daniel** and his immediate readers could not have comprehended all the details of the prophecies given in this book (cf. v. 8). Not until history continued to unfold would many be able to understand these prophetic revelations. But God indicated that an increased understanding of what Daniel had written would come. People today, looking back over history, can see the significance of much of what Daniel predicted. And in **the time of the end** (cf. v. 9 and note "the end" and "the end of the days" in v. 13) the words of this book that have been sealed (kept intact) will be understood by **many** who will seek to gain **knowledge** from it. This will be in the Tribulation (cf. 11:40, "the time of the end"). Even though Daniel's people may not have fully understood this book's prophecies, the predictions

---

[6] Anders, Max. *Holman Old Testament Commentary - Daniel* (p. 232). B&H Publishing.

did comfort them. They were assured that God will ultimately deliver Israel from the Gentiles and bring her into His covenanted promises."[7]

It is "the third year of Cyrus king of Persia," and hence about 536 B.C.E., shortly after the Jews' return to Jerusalem. After a three-week fast, Daniel is by the bank of the Hiddekel (the Tigris) river. (Dan. 10:1, 4; Gen. 2:14) An angel appears to him and explains

**Daniel 10:13-14** Updated American Standard Version (UASV)

13 The prince of the kingdom of Persia withstood me twenty-one days, but Michael, one of the chief princes, came to help me, for I was left there with the kings of Persia, **14** Now I have come to give you an understanding of what will happen to your people in the end of the days, for it is a vision yet for the days to come."

Chapter 10 of the book of Daniel precedes the final vision that was given to Daniel, the battles between The Kings of the South and the North.

**Daniel 11:1** Updated American Standard Version (UASV)

**11** "And as for me, in the first year of Darius the Mede [539/538 B.C.E.], I stood up to confirm and strengthen him.

This opening verse of chapter 11 could just as easily be seen as the closing verse of chapter 10. This is the angel still speaking here, not Daniel, and he is referring to his reign as the starting point of the prophetic message, as Darius was no longer living. God's angel continued,

**Daniel 11:2** Updated American Standard Version (UASV)

2 And now I will show you the truth. Behold, three more kings shall arise in Persia, and a fourth shall be far richer than all of them. And when he has become strong through his riches, he shall stir up all against the kingdom of Greece.

Just who were these Persian rulers?

---

[7] J. Dwight Pentecost, "Daniel," in *The Bible Knowledge Commentary: An Exposition of the Scriptures*, ed. J. F. Walvoord and R. B. Zuck, vol. 1 (Wheaton, IL: Victor Books, 1985), 1373.

As to whether the Jews remained God's chosen people after the rejection of Jesus Christ, the Son of God, see this author's CPH Blog article, MODERN ISRAEL IN BIBLE PROPHECY: Are the Natural Jews Today Still God's Chosen People?

https://christianpublishinghouse.co/2017/03/27/modern-israel-in-bible-prophecy-are-the-natural-jews-today-still-gods-chosen-people/

or http://tiny.cc/mdippy

The **three more kings shall arise in Persia** refer to Cyrus (539–529 B.C.E.), Cambyses (529–522 B.C.E.), and Darius I (Hystaspes) (521–486 B.C.), with Bardiya not being considered because he ruled for only seven months. The fourth was the son and successor of Darius, Xerxes I (485–465 B.C.). He was the King Ahasuerus who married Esther, who was richer than all who preceded him. With his wealth and power, he embarked on a campaign against Greece.

**Daniel 11:3-4** Updated American Standard Version (UASV)

[3] And a mighty king will arise, and he will rule with great dominion and do as he wills. [4] And as soon as he has **stood up,**[8] his kingdom shall be broken and divided toward the four winds of heaven, but not to **his posterity, nor according to the authority** with which he ruled, for his kingdom shall be plucked up and go to others besides these.

Twenty-year-old Alexander "**stood up**" as king of Macedonia in 336 B.C.E. He did become "a mighty king," known the world over today as Alexander the Great. "Between 334 and 330 B. Alexander conquered Asia Minor, Syria, Egypt, and the land of the Medo-Persian Empire. His conquests extended as far as India."[9] Alexander was not quite 33 years old when malaria coupled with alcoholism took his life in Babylon in 323 B.C.E.

The great empire of Alexander the Great was not passed onto "**his posterity**." Alexander's brother Philip III Arrhidaeus reign lasted less than seven years, as he and his wife Eurydice were murdered at the order of Olympias, Alexander's mother, in 317 B.C.E. Alexander's son Alexander IV ruled until 311 B.C.E., wherein he was killed at the hands of Cassander, one of his father's generals. Alexander has an illegitimate son Heracles, who then sought to rule in his father's name but was murdered in 309 B.C.E. Thus, we see that Alexander the Great rose up as a mighty king and ruled with great dominion, yet his kingdom was short lived but was not to go to his posterity because they could not rule with his authority.

Rather Alexander's kingdom was literally "broken and divided toward the four winds of heaven," that is, "his kingdom was divided among his four generals (cf. 8:22): Seleucus (over Syria and Mesopotamia), Ptolemy (over Egypt), Lysimacus (over Thrace and portions of Asia Minor), and Cassander

---

[8] Or *risen*

[9] J. Dwight Pentecost, "Daniel," in *The Bible Knowledge Commentary: An Exposition of the Scriptures*, ed. J. F. Walvoord and R. B. Zuck, vol. 1 (Wheaton, IL: Victor Books, 1985), 1367–1368.

(over Macedonia and Greece). This division was anticipated through the four heads of the leopard (7:6) and the four prominent horns on the goat (8:8)."[10]

**Daniel 11:5-6** Updated American Standard Version (UASV)

**5** "Then the king of the south will be strong, but one of his princes will be stronger than he and will rule, and his authority will be a greater dominion. **6** After some years they will make an alliance, and the daughter of the king of the south will come to the king of the north to make an agreement. But she will not retain the strength of her arm, and he and his arm will not endure, but she will be given up, along with those who brought her in, he who fathered her, and he who supported her in those times.

The titles "the king of the south" and "the king of the north" refer to kings south and north of Daniel's people, who had been freed from Babylonian captivity and was now restored to the land of Judah. The first "king of the south" was a general who had served under Alexander, Ptolemy I Soter of Egypt (304-283 B.C.E.). Another general of Alexander was Syrian King Seleucus I Nicator (304-281 B.C.E) "and his authority will be a greater dominion," who assumed the role of "the king of the north."

From the initial "king of the south" and the "king of the north" "conflicts arose between the kingdoms of the Ptolemies (Egypt) and the Seleucids (Syria)."[11] Because Antiochus I, the son and successor of his father Seleucus I Nicator did not wage a significant war against the king of the south, the prophecy did not mention him. However, his successor, Antiochus II, fought a very long war against Ptolemy II, the son of Ptolemy I. Therefore, Ptolemy II and Antiochus II constituted the king of the south and the king of the north respectively. Antiochus II married Laodice, and they had a son named Seleucus II, while Ptolemy II had a daughter named Berenice. In about 250 B.C.E., "the daughter of the king of the south will come to the king of the north to make an agreement." In order to make this alliance, Antiochus II divorced his wife Laodice and married Berenice, "the daughter of the king of the south."

We are told (11:6) she will not retain the strength of her arm, that is the supporting power of her father, Ptolemy II. When he died in 246 B.C.E., she did no longer had the support and power of her father, as his "arm will not endure" with her husband. Bernice "will be given up, along with those who

[10] J. Dwight Pentecost, "Daniel," in *The Bible Knowledge Commentary: An Exposition of the Scriptures*, ed. J. F. Walvoord and R. B. Zuck, vol. 1 (Wheaton, IL: Victor Books, 1985), 1368.

[11] Stephen R. Miller, *Daniel*, vol. 18, The New American Commentary (Nashville: Broadman & Holman Publishers, 1994), 293.

brought her in, he who fathered her, and he who supported her in those times.

But and he and his arm will not endure, but she shall be given up, along with those who brought her in, he who fathered her, and he who supported her in those times. Antiochus II rejected Bernice; after that, he remarried Laodice and named their son as his successor. As Laodice had planned, she succeeded "in murdering Antiochus, Berenice, and their child. Thus their 'power' did 'not last.' Laodice then ruled as queen regent during the minority of her son, Seleucus II Callinicus (246–226 B.C.)."[12] J. Dwight Pentecost tells us, "Laodice, whom Antiochus had divorced in order to marry Berenice, had Berenice killed (she was **handed over**). Laodice then poisoned Antiochus II and made her son, Seleucus II Callinicus, king (246–227)."[13] How would the next Ptolemaic king respond to all of this?

**Daniel 11:7-9** Updated American Standard Version (UASV)

7 "And **one from the sprout of her roots** will stand up in his position, and he will come to the army and come against **the fortress of the king of the north**, and he will deal with them and will prevail. 8 Also their gods, with their **metal images,**[14] with their precious vessels of silver and of gold, he will take captive to Egypt; and for some years he will stand off from the king of the north, 9 Then the latter will come into the realm of the king of the south but will return to his own land.

"One from the sprout" of Berenice's parents, or "roots," was her brother. At his father's death, he 'stood up' as the king of the south, the Egyptian Pharaoh Ptolemy III Euergetes (246–221 B.C.E.). He wasted no time in the vengeance of his sister's murder. He attacked Syrian King Seleucus II, who Laodice had used to murder Berenice and her son, he came against "the fortress of the king of the north." Ptolemy III took the fortified part of Antioch, capturing the major cities of Antioch and Seleucia and dealt a deathblow to Laodice.

Some 200 years earlier, Persian King Cambyses II had conquered Egypt and carried home Egyptian gods, "their metal images" or "their molten statues." Here we have Ptolemy III plundering the former royal capital Susa, where he recovered these "gods," taking them captive, carrying home the spoils of war. He also brought back as spoils of war a great many "precious

---

[12] IBID, 293–294.

[13] J. Dwight Pentecost, "Daniel," in *The Bible Knowledge Commentary: An Exposition of the Scriptures*, ed. J. F. Walvoord and R. B. Zuck, vol. 1 (Wheaton, IL: Victor Books, 1985), 1368.

[14] Or *molten statues*

vessels of silver and of gold." And Ptolemy III "for some years he will stand off from the king of the north," to quell revolt at home.

However, the king of the north, Syrian King Seleucus II, attempted to strike back. "In 242 Seleucus II attempted to invade Egypt but was forced to withdraw. For the rest of his reign, he was too busy with other problems to engage in further conflict with Egypt."[15] Seleucus II with only a small remnant of his army was forced to "return to his own land." At his death, his son Seleucus III succeeded him. "This was the beginning of the seesaw battle between the two nations."[16]

---

[15] John H Walton, *Zondervan Illustrated Bible Backgrounds Commentary (Old Testament): Isaiah, Jeremiah, Lamentations, Ezekiel, Daniel*, vol. 4 (Grand Rapids, MI: Zondervan, 2009), 562.

[16] Walvoord, John. Daniel (The John Walvoord Prophecy Commentaries) (Kindle Location 6113). Moody Publishers.

# CHAPTER 2 The Kings of the South and the North - Daniel 11:10-20 (226 - 175 B.C.E.)

**Daniel 11:10-13** Updated American Standard Version (UASV)

10 "His sons will wage war and assemble a multitude of great forces, which will keep coming and overflow and pass through, and again will wage war up to his fortress. 11 Then the king of the south, moved with rage, will come out and fight against the king of the north. And he will raise a great multitude, but it will be given into his hand. 12 And when the multitude is **taken away**, his heart will be lifted up, and he will cast down tens of thousands, but he will not prevail. 13 For the king of the north will again raise a multitude, greater than the former, and after some years[17] he will come on with a great army and many supplies.

Seleucus III reign was short-lived, for in less than three years he was assassinated. His brother, Antiochus III, came to the Syrian throne. After he had dealt with the rebellions in Media and Asia Minor, Antiochus III gathered a great military force for an attack on the king of the south, who was by then Ptolemy IV. "Antiochus III … was called the "Great" because of his military successes, and in 219–218 B.C. he campaigned in Phoenicia and Palestine, part of the Ptolemaic Empire ("as far as his [the king of the South's] fortress")."[18]

Massing a military force of 75,000, the king of the south, Ptolemy IV, moved northward against the enemy, the king of the north. We are told that the Syrian king of the north, Antiochus III raised "a great multitude [68,000], but it will be given into his hand." Antiochus III suffered defeat at the coastal city of Raphia, not far from Egypt's border.[19] A "multitude is taken away" by Ptolemy IV, the king of the south, 10,000 Syrian infantrymen and 300 cavalrymen into death and he took 4,000 as prisoners. The kings then made a truce agreement whereby Antiochus III kept his Syrian seaport of Seleucia but lost Phoenicia and Coele-Syria. Because of this victory, the 'heart of the

---

[17] Lit *at the end of the times, years*

[18] Stephen R. Miller, *Daniel*, vol. 18, The New American Commentary (Nashville: Broadman & Holman Publishers, 1994), 294.

[19] "According to Polybius, Ptolemy's forces consisted of 70,000 infantry, 5,000 cavalry, and 73 elephants; whereas Antiochus's army had 62,000 infantry, 6,000 cavalry, and 102 elephants. When the battle ended [in 217 B.C.], Ptolemy had won a great victory over the Syrians at Raphia (located in Palestine)." – Stephen R. Miller, Daniel, vol. 18, The New American Commentary (Nashville: Broadman & Holman Publishers, 1994), 295.

Egyptian king of the south was lifted up,' especially toward the one true God of the Jews. Judah remained under the control of Ptolemy IV. Nevertheless, he did not take advantage of the strong position that he held, trying to stay on top of this victory against the Syrian king of the north, so in the end 'he did not prevail.

But rather, Ptolemy IV turned to a life of depravity and corruption, and his five-year-old son, Ptolemy V, became the next king of the south some years before the death of Antiochus III. "fifteen years later (202 b.c.) Antiochus III again invaded Ptolemaic territories with a huge army. The occasion for this invasion was the death of Ptolemy IV in 203 B.C. and the crowning of his young son (between four and six years of age), Ptolemy V Epiphanes (203–181 B.C.), as the new king. Antiochus III took full advantage of the opportunity and attacked Phoenicia and Palestine; by 201 B.C. the fortress in Gaza had fallen to the Syrians."[20]

**Daniel 11:14** Updated American Standard Version (UASV)

**14** "In those times many will rise against the king of the south, and the **violent among your own people** will lift themselves up in order to fulfill the vision, but they will stumble.[21]

"In those times many [did] rise against the king of the south." Not only did the king of the south have to face the forces of Antiochus III, as well as his Macedonian ally, but the young king also had many problems at home in Egypt. The young king of the south was facing a revolt because his guardian Agathocles, who ruled in his name, dealt haughtily with the Egyptians. Daniel 11:14b tells us "the violent among your own people will lift themselves up in order to fulfill the vision." However, this "vision" of ending the Gentile dominion of their homeland was false and they 'were going to stumble.'

**Daniel 11:15-16** Updated American Standard Version (UASV)

**15** And the king of the north will come and throw up a siege rampart and capture a **fortified city**. And the arms of the south will not stand, nor will his select men; and they will have no power to stand. **16** The one coming against him will do as he pleases, and no one will stand before him; he will **stand in the land of the beauty,**[22] with destruction in his hand.

---

[20] Stephen R. Miller, *Daniel*, vol. 18, The New American Commentary (Nashville: Broadman & Holman Publishers, 1994), 295.

[21] Or *will fail*

[22] I.e. Palestine

Military forces under Ptolemy V, or "arms of the south," surrendered to assault from the north. At Paneas (Caesarea Philippi), Antiochus III drove Egypt's General Scopas and 10,000 "select men," into Sidon, "a fortified city." There Antiochus III would "throw up a siege rampart," taking that Phoenician seaport in 199 B.C.E. "He then retreated to Sidon on the Phoenician coast. Antiochus's forces pursued the Egyptians and besieged Sidon. General Scopas finally surrendered in 198 B.C.E."[23] Antiochus would "do as he pleases" because "no one [the Egyptian king of the south] will stand before him." Antiochus III then marched against Jerusalem, the capital of "the land of the beauty," namely, Judah, "with destruction in his hand."

**Daniel 11:17** Updated American Standard Version (UASV)

[17] He will **set his face** to come **with the full force of his kingdom**, and there will be **equitable terms**; and he will perform them; he will give him the daughter of women to destroy her. But she will not stand for him, or be for him.

The king of the north, Antiochus III, "set his face" to completely control Egypt "with the full force of his kingdom." But rather he chose in the end to make "equitable terms" of peace with the king of the south, Ptolemy V. When Antiochus III and King Philip V of Macedonia join in a league or alliance against the young Egyptian king, attempting to take over his territories, the guardians of Ptolemy V went to Rome for protection, causing Antiochus III to change his plan. In this alliance of peace Antiochus III gave his daughter, Cleopatra I "the daughter of women," in marriage to Ptolemy V, hoping his daughter would be an inside spy so as to make Egypt subject to Syria. However, the scheme failed because Cleopatra I "[would] not stand for him, or be for him," but rather she sided with her husband. She "became staunchly loyal to her husband, even encouraging him to make an alliance with Rome against her father."[24]

Gleason L. Archer offers insight into this masterful scheme gone bad, "As it turned out, however, after the marriage finally took place in 195 [B.C.E.], Cleopatra became completely sympathetic to her husband, Ptolemy V, and the Ptolemaic cause, much to the disappointment of her father, Antiochus. Therefore, when she gave birth to a royal heir, who became Ptolemy VI, this gave no particular advantage or political leverage to her

---

[23] Stephen R. Miller, *Daniel*, vol. 18, The New American Commentary (Nashville: Broadman & Holman Publishers, 1994), 296.

[24] John H Walton, *Zondervan Illustrated Bible Backgrounds Commentary (Old Testament): Isaiah, Jeremiah, Lamentations, Ezekiel, Daniel*, vol. 4 (Grand Rapids, MI: Zondervan, 2009), 564.

father. When Ptolemy V died in 181, Cleopatra was appointed queen regent by the Egyptian government, because they all loved and appreciated her loyalty to their cause. But she herself died not long after, and this meant the end of all possible Seleucid influence on Egyptian affairs. Yet by that time Antiochus himself, who died in 187 B.C., was gone." (Archer, The Expositor's Bible Commentary, Vol. 7: Daniel and the Minor Prophets 1985, 132-33)

**Daniel 11:18-19** Updated American Standard Version (UASV)

18 Afterward he will **turn his face back to the coastlands** and will capture many. But a **commander** will put a stop to his reproach against him; he will turn his reproach upon him. 19 Then he will turn his face back toward the fortresses of his own land, but he will stumble and fall, and will not be found.

Antiochus would "turn his face back to the coastlands. The "coastlands" were those of Macedonia, Greece, and Asia Minor. Antiochus is an effort to repeat the accomplishments of Alexander the Great, sought to conquer and control Greece. However, Greece had other plans, as they turned to Rome for help. Rome formally declared war on him. This put Antiochus in battle on several fronts: Macedonia, Rome, and Greece. "The Romans defeated [Antiochus] at Thermopylae in 191 [B.C.E.] and then crushed him at the Battle of Magnesia in 190 [B.C.E.]. This forced him back east across the Taurus Mountains. The commander who defeated him was Lucius Scipio. By the Treaty of Apmea in 189 [B.C.E.] Antiochus became a vassal of Rome, had to send twenty hostages to Rome, and paid a huge indemnity. This left him humiliated and short of funds."[25]

**Daniel 11:20** Updated American Standard Version (UASV)

20 "Then there will stand up in his position one who causes an exactor to pass through the glory of his kingdom, but in a few days he will be broken, though not in anger nor in warfare.

God's angel foretold, "There will stand up in his position [***that of Antiochus III***] one who causes an exactor [the tax collector Heliodorus] to pass through the glory of his kingdom, but in a few days, he will be broken, though not in anger nor in warfare." (Daniel 11:20) The one who was to "standing up" in this manner was Seleucus IV Philopator. (187–175 B.C.E.) "Seleucus IV reigned only 'a few years' and was not killed by an angry mob ("in anger") like his father or 'in battle.' Heliodorus, his tax collector and

[25] John H Walton, *Zondervan Illustrated Bible Backgrounds Commentary (Old Testament): Isaiah, Jeremiah, Lamentations, Ezekiel, Daniel*, vol. 4 (Grand Rapids, MI: Zondervan, 2009), 564.

prime minister, evidently seeking to gain the throne for himself, poisoned the king (possibly abetted by Antiochus IV)."[26]

[26] Stephen R. Miller, *Daniel*, vol. 18, The New American Commentary (Nashville: Broadman & Holman Publishers, 1994), 297.

# CHAPTER 3 The Kings of the South and the North - Daniel 11:21-35 (175 - 164 B.C.E.)

**Daniel 11:21** Updated American Standard Version (UASV)

21 And there will stand up in his place **a despicable one**, and they have not conferred the majesty of the kingdom; and he will come in during a time of security and seize the kingdom by intrigue.

Antiochus IV Epiphanes (175–163 B.C.E.) had been a political hostage in Rome Since the defeat of Antiochus III at Magnesia. However, in 175 B.C.E. the oldest son of Seleucus IV, Demetrius I, was sent to Rome in replacement of Antiochus IV. Arriving home, Antiochus IV assumed power as a co-ruler with Antiochus III, the latter here dying in 170 C.E., leaving Antiochus IV to rule alone on the throne. Antiochus IV Epiphanes was certainly "a despicable one," for his severe persecution of the Jews, massacring thousands, and he became the greatest threat to the pure worship within Israel since Abraham left Haran for the Promise Land. Antiochus IV assumed the title Epiphanes, which means the "Manifest One," or "Illustrious One," clearly evidencing his haughty spirit.

**Daniel 11:22-24** Updated American Standard Version (UASV)

22 Armies shall be **utterly swept away** before him and broken, even **the leader of the covenant.** 23 And after an alliance is made with him, he will act deceitfully, and he will rise and he will become powerful by means of a little nation. 24 **In a time of tranquility** he will enter the richest parts of the province, and he will accomplish what his fathers and their fathers have not done; he will distribute plunder, booty and possessions among them, and he will **devise his schemes against strongholds**, but only for a time.

At the tender age of six Ptolemy VII (Philometor) took the throne at the age of six under control of his mother Cleopatra in 181 B.C.E., as it was she who controlled the kingdom. Shortly after that he moves on Palestine with a huge military force and was soundly defeated by Antiochus Epiphanes who destroyed, in the process, "the leader of the covenant." The Egyptian armies were utterly swept away by the invading forces of Antiochus as if it were by a flood. Antiochus gave the order to murder "the leader of the covenant, Onias III, which was carried out by his own defecting brother Menelaus about 171 B.C.E.

Walvoord tells us, "The reference to the "prince of the covenant" prophesied the deposing and eventual murder of the high priest Onias, which was ordered by Antiochus in 172 B.C. and indicates the troublesome times of his reign.39 The high priest bore the title "prince of the covenant" because he was de facto the head of the theocracy at that time. In 11:28 and 11:32 the term "covenant" is used for the Jewish state. Antiochus sold the office of high priest to Onias's brother, Jason, who sought to Hellenize the Jewish state."[27]

However, Stephen R. Miller sees the "prince of the covenant differently, saying, "Montgomery identifies the "prince [leader] of the covenant" as the high priest Onias III, who was assassinated in 170 B.C. (Daniel, 451; also, Lacocque, Daniel, 226; Hartman and Di Lella, Daniel, 295; Wood, Daniel, 295). In context with the defeat of the Egyptian army, it is best to see this "prince" as its leader. The entire phrase is indefinite and can be rendered 'a prince of a covenant.' He goes on to say, "Ptolemy is called 'a prince [leader] of the covenant' because he agreed (made a covenant) to become an ally of Antiochus if the Syrians would help him regain his throne in Egypt, which had been taken by his younger brother, Ptolemy VII Euergetes II (Physcon). Antiochus was delighted to make such a pact, for he felt that it would give him a foothold in Egypt. So with Syrian help, Ptolemy regained his throne. Later Ptolemy broke this agreement and allied himself with his brother Ptolemy VII to dislodge Antiochus's troops from Pelusium, a fortress on the border of Egypt."[28]

In verse 24 we find Antiochus Epiphanes taking from the rich Egyptian places he could strike and giving to the poor and his own forces, to gain support and strengthen his control over the empire, as well as build up to take over Egypt.

**Daniel 11:25-28** Updated American Standard Version (UASV)

**25** And he will **stir up his power and his heart against the king of the south** with a great army; and the king of the south shall wage war with an exceedingly great and mighty army, but he will not stand, for plots will be devised against him. **26** Even **those who eat** his food will break him; and his army will be swept away, and many will fall down slain. **27** As for both kings, their heart will be inclined to do what is evil, and **they will speak lies** to each other at the same table; but it will not succeed, for the end is still to come at the appointed time. **28** Then he will return to his land with many possessions,

---

[27] Walvoord, John. Daniel (The John Walvoord Prophecy Commentaries) (Kindle Locations 6232-6237). Moody Publishers.

[28] Stephen R. Miller, *Daniel*, vol. 18, The New American Commentary (Nashville: Broadman & Holman Publishers, 1994), 299.

but his heart will be set **against the holy covenant**, and he will take action and he will return to his own land.

Antiochus set out to attacked Ptolemy VI Philometer in 170 B.C.E., the king of Egypt (c. 186 – 145 B.C.E.), who had become his enemy. Antiochus was able to defeat an Egyptian army near Pelusium, and then he captured Memphis but was not in a position to take Alexandria. Miller tells us that "Cumulatively these things prevented Ptolemy from successfully 'standing' against the Syrians. 'Those who eat from the king's provisions' (v. 26) were Ptolemy's trusted counselors, who unwisely urged the young king to recapture Syria and Palestine, thus incurring the wrath of Antiochus."[29]

Antiochus Epiphanes 'spoke lies,' as he pretended to help Ptolemy Philometer regain the throne in Egypt, which was then by Ptolemy Euergetes. Both kings "they will speak lies to each other at the same table." Antiochus had Philometer as king at Memphis, while he had Euergetes reigned at Alexandria. However, things did not go as planned because the two Egyptian kings decided up a joint rule, which greatly angered the Syrian. "Antiochus's successful first campaign against Egypt in 169 B.C. is the background for v. 28. After plundering Egypt, the king returned home by way of Palestine and found an insurrection in progress (cf. 1 Macc. 1:16–28; 2 Macc. 5:1–11). He put down the rebellion, massacring eighty thousand men, women, and children (2 Macc. 5:12–14) and then looted the temple with the help of the evil high priest, Menelaus (cf. 2 Macc. 5:15–21). The persecution of the Jews by this evil tyrant had now escalated to calamitous proportions."[30] These sources outside of the Scriptures are not inspired books of the Bible. However, First and Second Maccabees are historical accounts of the Jewish struggle for independence during the second-century B.C.E. These are the most valuable of the Old Testament Apocryphal works because of the historical information they supply for this period.

**Daniel 11:29-30** Updated American Standard Version (UASV)

**29** "At the appointed time he will return and he will **come into the south**, but it will not be as it was before. **30** For **ships** of Kittim[31] will **come against him**; therefore he will be disheartened and will return and become

[29] Stephen R. Miller, *Daniel*, vol. 18, The New American Commentary (Nashville: Broadman & Holman Publishers, 1994), 300.

[30] Stephen R. Miller, *Daniel*, vol. 18, The New American Commentary (Nashville: Broadman & Holman Publishers, 1994), 300.

[31] I.e. Cyprus

enraged at the holy covenant and take action; so he will come back and show regard for those who forsake the holy covenant.

Here again, for the third time, we find Antiochus invading Egypt against the co-rulers about 168 B.C.E., "but it will not be as it was before, for a Roman fleet of ships from Cyprus sided with Egypt this time, frustrating the attack by Antiochus. "When he tried to play for time, the Roman envoy drew a circle around him in the sand and insisted on an answer before he stepped out of it. Humiliated, he withdrew from Egypt."[32] Antiochus left Egypt in a fit of rage, taking his anger out on the Israelites as he headed back home. He despised the Jews God and their Mosaic Law, so he showed favor to the apostate Jews, yes Antiochus showed "regard for those who forsake the holy covenant."

Miller tells us that "In 167 B.C., Antiochus turned his humiliation into anger against the Jewish people ("the holy covenant") once more (cf. 1 Macc 1:29–40; 2 Macc 6:1–6). He sent Apollonius (2 Macc 5:23–26), the head of his mercenaries and the "chief collector of tribute" (1 Macc 1:29), to Jerusalem. Apollonius pretended to come in peace, but on the Sabbath Day, he suddenly attacked, massacring many people and plundering the city (cf. 1 Macc. 1:30–32; cf. 2 Macc. 5:25–26). But he rewarded those apostate Jews like the high priest Menelaus, who supported his Hellenistic policies (cf. 1 Macc. 1:1, 43; 2 Macc. 4:7–17)."[33]

**Daniel 11:31-32** Updated American Standard Version (UASV)

**31** Forces from him will stand up, **desecrate the sanctuary** fortress, and do away with the continual sacrifice. And they will set up the **abomination[34] that causes desolation.** **32** And those who act wickedly against the covenant, he will pollute by means of smooth words; but **the people who know their God** will prevail and act effectively.

The soldier of Antiochus worked in conjunction with the apostate Jews, guarding the temple, halting pure worship of the one true God. In addition, other Antiochus troops were sent out on the Sabbath to slaughter Jewish men, women, and children. The soldiers "desecrate the sanctuary," banned circumcision, and done away with away with "the continual sacrifice" (i.e.,

---

[32] John H Walton, *Zondervan Illustrated Bible Backgrounds Commentary (Old Testament): Isaiah, Jeremiah, Lamentations, Ezekiel, Daniel*, vol. 4 (Grand Rapids, MI: Zondervan, 2009), 565.

[33] Stephen R. Miller, *Daniel*, vol. 18, The New American Commentary (Nashville: Broadman & Holman Publishers, 1994), 301.

[34] **Abomination**: (Heb. *shiqquts*) It means abhorrence, an object to abhor, horror, monster, filth. The sense of *shiqquts* is a detestable thing, also implying that it can make a person unclean. – 2 Ki 23:13; Ez. 5:11; 11:21; Dan. 9:27; 11:31; Hos. 9:10.

daily sacrifices), as well as offering up in sacrifice a big on God's altar. (1 Macc. 1:44–54) Moreover, on Chislev (Dec. 15, 167 B.C.E.) the Syrians even made compulsory worship of an idol statue in honor of the Olympian god Zeus in the temple. The Jews called it "the abomination that causes desolation." **Abomination**: (Heb. *shiqquts*) It means abhorrence, an object to abhor, horror, monster, filth. The sense of *shiqquts* is a detestable thing, also implying that it can make a person unclean. In other words, the Syrians ruined pure worship of the one true God in the temple by introducing an abhorrent, detestable, filthy object (the Olympian god Zeus) in the temple. The soldiers of Antiochus further profaned the temple by spreading sow's broth on the altar. (1 Macc. 1:44-54) Both Daniel and Jesus said this barbarism was only a preview of the abomination that was to come – Daniel 9:27; Matthew 24:15.

**The Abomination of Desolation**

**Matthew 24:15** Updated American Standard Version (UASV)

**15** "Therefore when you see the abomination of desolation, which was spoken of through Daniel the prophet, standing in the holy place (let the reader understand),

Matthew 24:13 reads, "But **the one who endures to the end** will be saved." Matthew 24:14 said, "this gospel of the kingdom will be proclaimed throughout the whole world as a testimony to all nations, **and then the end will come**." Matthew 24:15 begins with the Greek word *hotan* "whenever" followed by *oun* "therefore, which reads in English, "Therefore when," which connects what preceded, "**the end**," and leads into what follows. Let us take a moment to investigate verse 15.

In verse 3-14, Jesus outlined the signs of "the end of the age." Here in Mathew 24:15, Jesus begins with "**Therefore when** you see the abomination of desolation, which was spoken of through Daniel the prophet, standing in the holy place (let the reader understand)." If we look at the corresponding accounts in Mark and Luke, they offer us additional insights. Mark 13:14 says, "standing where it ought not to be." Luke 21:20 adds Jesus' words, "But when you see Jerusalem surrounded by armies, then know[35] that its desolation has come near." The complete picture is an "abomination" "standing in the holy place," i.e., "where it ought not be," namely, "Jerusalem surrounded by armies,"

This is a reference to the Roman army, which assaulted Jerusalem and its temple starting in 66 C.E., under General Cestus Gallus. The temple was the "holy place," and the abomination was the Roman army "standing where

[35] Or *then recognize*

it ought not to be." As for the "desolation," this came in 70 C.E. when General Titus of the Roman army completely desolated Jerusalem and its temple. Specifically, what was this "abomination"? Moreover, in what sense was it "standing in the holy place"?

Jesus had urged the readers to *understand.* What was it that they were to *understand*? They were to *understand* that "which was spoken of through Daniel the prophet," i.e., Daniel 9:27. Part "b" of verse 27 reads "And upon the wing of abominations shall come the one causing desolation, even until a complete destruction, one that is decreed, is poured out on the one causing desolation." – Daniel 9:26-27; see also Daniel 11:31; 12:11.

> The *abomination of desolation* is an expression that recurs in Daniel with some variation in wording (Daniel 8:13; 9:27; 11:31; 12:11), where most scholars agree that there is a reference to the desecration perpetrated by Antiochus Epiphanes when he built an altar to Zeus in the temple and offered swine and other unclean animals on it as sacrifices (cf. 1 Macc. 1:41–61).[36]

*STANDARD OF THE 10TH ROMAN LEGION This Legion attacked and destroyed Jerusalem in the Jewish War (A.D. 70).*

We can have it but one of two ways, as Jesus' words were a clear reference to the Roman armies of 66–70 C.E. It may very well be that Daniel's prophecy points to Antiochus Epiphanes "who in 167 [B.C.E., 200-years before Jesus uttered his prophecy] plundered the temple, ordered the sacrificial system to cease, and polluted the altar of the Lord by turning it into a pagan altar, where unclean sacrifices were offered to pagan deities."[37] This would be no different from Matthew referring to Hosea 11:1 (When Israel was a child … and out of Egypt I called my son). In that case, Matthew did not use Hosea's intended meaning, but carried out an *Inspired Sensus Plenior Application*, by having a whole other meaning, an entirely different meaning for those words, making them applicable to Jesus being called back out of Egypt. It could be that Jesus used Daniel's prophecy about Antiochus Epiphanes, and gave is an *Inspired Sensus Plenior Application*, by having a whole other meaning, a completely different meaning for those words, making them applicable to

---

[36] Leon Morris, *The Gospel According to Matthew*, The Pillar New Testament Commentary (Grand Rapids, MI; Leicester, England: W.B. Eerdmans; Inter-Varsity Press, 1992), 603.

[37] Larry Chouinard, *Matthew*, The College Press NIV Commentary (Joplin, MO: College Press, 1997), Mt 24:15.

the Roman armies desolating Jerusalem between 66 and 70 C.E. Then, again, it could be that was what Daniel was pointing to all along, and Jesus used Daniel's words in a grammatical-historical application. Either way, it still comes out the same.

> During the days of the Maccabees this expression was used to describe the sacrilege of Antiochus IV Epiphanes, the Seleucid king who decreed that an altar to Olympian Zeus and perhaps a statue of himself were to be erected in the temple on 15 Chislev, 167 b.c.: "They erected a desolating sacrilege on the altar of burnt offering. They also built altars in the surrounding towns of Judah." Antiochus further decreed that the Sabbath and other festal observances were to be profaned, that circumcision was to be abolished, and that swine and other unclean animals were to be sacrificed in the temple (cf. 1 Macc. 1:41–50). This was one of the lowest points of Jewish history and was considered by many the primary focus of Daniel's prophecy. Jesus now quotes Daniel directly to clarify that the fulfillment of the "abomination that causes desolation" is yet future.[38]

When Jesus uttered those words of verse 15, the abomination of desolation was yet to appear. Jesus was clearly pointing to the Roman army of 66 C.E., with its distinctive standards, which were idols to the Romans and the empire, but an abomination to the Jews.

Judæa was under the charge of a Roman official, a subordinate of the governor of the Roman province of Syria, who held a relation to that functionary similar to that which the Governor of Bombay holds to the Governor-General at Calcutta. Roman soldiers paraded the streets of Jerusalem; **Roman standards** waved over the fastnesses of the country; Roman tax-gatherers sat at the gate of every town. To the Sanhedrin, the supreme Jewish organ of government, only a shadow of power was still conceded, its presidents, the high priests, being mere puppets of Rome, set up and put down with the utmost caprice. So low had the proud nation fallen whose ideal it had ever been to rule the world, and whose patriotism was a religious and national passion as intense and unquenchable as ever burned in any country.[39]

In verse 32 we are told "but the people who know their God will prevail and act effectively," which referred to the Hasmonaeans. A dynamic Jewish

---

[38] Clinton E. Arnold, *Zondervan Illustrated Bible Backgrounds Commentary: Matthew, Mark, Luke*, vol. 1 (Grand Rapids, MI: Zondervan, 2002), 148.

[39] James Stalker, *The Life of Jesus Christ* (Chicago: Henry A. Sumner and Company, 1882), 30–31.

leader, Judah Maccabee, of a family known as the Hasmonaeans, led a rebel army that freed the temple from Greek hands. Possibly because of Judah's military ability, he was called Maccabee, meaning "hammer." Maccabee was a "name given to the family of Mattathias, a faithful priest, who led in a revolt (Maccabean War) against the Hellenizing influences of the Seleucid King Antiochus Epiphanes in about 168 B.C.E."[40]

**The Hasmonaean Dynasty**

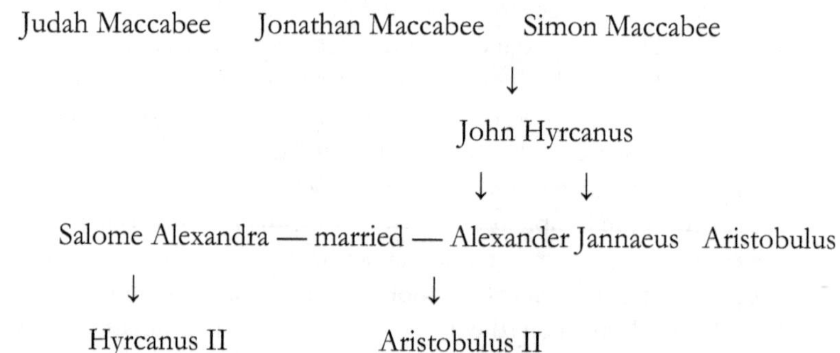


**II. Maccabean Revolt**

A. Antiochus's Revenge (168–166 B.C.) In the winter of 169/168, the rival brothers Ptolemy VI and Ptolemy VIII agreed to end their dispute and united against their uncle Antiochus IV. Thus, in the spring of 168 Antiochus IV invaded Egypt a second time. He captured Memphis, but when he attempted to subdue Eleusis, a suburb of Alexandria, the Roman general Popillius Laenas gave him an ultimatum from the senate to withdraw immediately from Egypt (cf. Polybius xxix.2.1–4; 27.1–8; Livy xlv.12.1–6; Diodorus xxxi.2; Velleius Paterculus i.10.1f; Appian Syr 66; Justinus xxxiv.3; Dnl. 11:28–30). Antiochus immediately retreated, having learned of Rome's power as its hostage for fourteen years.

Embittered, Antiochus decided to establish Palestine as a buffer state between him and the Roman encroachment (Polybius xxix.27.9; Dnl. 11:30). He destroyed the walls of Jerusalem and refortified the old Davidic city making it the pagan stronghold (Acra). Considering himself Zeus

[40] Chad Brand et al., eds., "Maccabees," *Holman Illustrated Bible Dictionary* (Nashville, TN: Holman Bible Publishers, 2003), 1063.

Epiphanes, he ordered a vigorous hellenization program that would exterminate the Jewish religion. He forbade the Jews to celebrate the sabbath and feasts, to offer the traditional sacrifices, and to perform circumcision, and he ordered the destruction of the copies of the Torah.

The Jews were ordered to offer up unclean sacrifices on idolatrous altars and to eat swine's flesh (2 Macc. 6:18). The climactic act was on 25 Chislev (Dec. 16) 167, when the temple of Jerusalem became the place of worship of the Olympian Zeus. The altar of Zeus was erected on the altar of burnt offering, and swine's flesh was offered on it (Dnl. 11:31f.; 1 Macc. 1:41–64; 2 Macc. 6:1–11).

B. Mattathias (166 B.C.) In every village of Palestine sacrifice was to be offered to the heathen gods under the supervision of imperial representatives. In the village of Modein (27 km, 17 mi, NW of Jerusalem) an aged priest named Mattathias defied the command of Antiochus IV's legate to offer the sacrifice on the heathen altar. When another Jew was about to comply, Mattathias killed him and the legate and destroyed the altar, saying, "Let everyone who is zealous for the law and supports the covenant come out with me" (1 Macc. 2:15–27; Josephus Ant. xii.6.1f [265–272]; cf. Dnl. 11:32–35). Mattathias, his five sons (John, Simon, Judas, Eleazar, and Jonathan) and many other Jews fled to the mountains; this marked the beginning of the Maccabean revolt.

Mattathias and his followers exhorted Jews everywhere to join their struggle against hellenization. They gained the support of the Hasidim, those who were faithful to the Torah. They tore down heathen altars and circumcised children who had been left uncircumcised. After a long life, Mattathias died in 166. He exhorted his sons to continue the struggle and appointed his third son Judas as the commander of the war (1 Macc. 2:42–70; Josephus Ant. xii.6.2–4 [273–286]).

C. Judas Maccabeus (166–160 B.C.)

1. Rededication of the Temple (166–164 B.C.) The selection of Judas to carry on the struggle was the right one, for he proved to be a very capable leader in defeating the Seleucids. In his first year he defeated the Syrian governors Apollonius and Seron (1 Macc. 3:10–26; Josephus Ant. xii.7.1 [287–292]).

Part of Antiochus's inability to put down the Maccabees was caused by the trouble he had in the East, which prevented him from being involved in Judea himself. Instead, he ordered Lysias, regent of the western part of the empire (Syria), to stop the rebellion and to destroy the Jewish race (1 Macc. 3:32–36; Josephus Ant. xii.7.2 [295f]). Lysias sent a large army under the leadership of Ptolemy, Nicanor, and Gorgias. So confident they were of victory that traders went along to purchase Jewish slaves (1 Macc. 3:38–41). But Judas decisively defeated Gorgias at Emmaus, causing the Syrian soldiers to flee (1 Macc. 4:1–27; Josephus Ant. xii.7.4 [305–312]).

In 164 Lysias made one last attempt against the Jews by personally leading a larger army to attack Jerusalem from the south. Judas, however, completely defeated him in Beth-zur (24 km, 15 mi, S of Jerusalem). Lysias retreated, and Judas marched to Jerusalem and regained all of Jerusalem except the Acra. Having captured the temple mount, he destroyed the altar of the Olympian Zeus, built a new altar, rebuilt the temple, and selected a priest who had remained faithful to Yahweh. Thus on 25 Chislev (Dec. 14) 164, exactly three years after its desecration, the temple was rededicated and the daily sacrifices were restored (1 Macc. 4:36–59; 2 Macc. 10:1–8; Josephus Ant. xii.7.6f [316–326]). This event marked the beginning of the Jewish Feast of Dedication or Lights (Hanukkah). Judas then fortified the Jerusalem walls and the city of Beth-zur. This completed the first phase of the Maccabean struggle. The Maccabees could rejoice, for they had not experienced defeat.

2. Religious Freedom Gained (163 B.C.) Judas's victories made Judah reasonably secure. Two things, however, needed to be accomplished. First, although Judah was reasonably secure, it was felt that all the Jews of Palestine had to be independent from Antiochus's rule. After several campaigns this freedom was won.

Second, the Maccabees wanted to end Syrian control of the Acra in Jerusalem. The Syrian presence was a constant reminder of Antiochus's hellenization program intended to exterminate the Jewish religion. When Judas laid siege to the Acra in the spring or summer of 163, some Syrian soldiers and Hellenistic Jews escaped and went to Antioch for help (1 Macc. 6:18–27).

Antiochus IV died in 163 (Polybius xxxi.9.3f.; Josephus Ant. xii.9.1 [356–59]) and was succeeded by his nine-year-old son Antiochus V Eupator. Just before his death, Antiochus IV had appointed his friend Philip as the regent and guardian over Antiochus V. But Lysias claimed that these privileges had been given to him at an earlier date, and so he crowned Antiochus V (both he and Philip were in Antioch when Antiochus IV died). Because of the troubles in Jerusalem, Lysias with the boy-king went south and defeated Judas at Beth-zechariah (18 km, 11 mi, SW of Jerusalem). There Judas's youngest brother Eleazar was killed.

Lysias then laid siege to Jerusalem (1 Macc. 6:28–54). Judas faced severe food shortages (because it was the sabbatical year) and was about to be defeated. Lysias, however, received the news that Philip was marching from Persia to Syria to claim the boy-king Antiochus V and the kingdom; thus he was anxious to make a peace treaty with Judas. Judas agreed to tear down the walls of Jerusalem, and Lysias guaranteed religious freedom to the Jews (1 Macc. 6:55–63). The Jews, however, were still under the Seleucidian rule.

3. Political Freedom Attempted (162–160 B.C.) Having obtained religious freedom, Judas now wanted political freedom. To counteract his drive, the Seleucids strengthened the Hellenistic elements among the Jews. Lysias, it seems, appointed the high priest Alcimus (Jakim or Jehoakim) who, although of Aaronic descent, was ideologically a Hellenist (cf. 1 Macc. 7:14; 2 Macc. 14:3–7; Josephus Ant. xii.9.7 [384–88]; xx.10.3 [235]) and thus unacceptable to Judas.

Meanwhile in Syria, Demetrius I Soter, nephew of Antiochus IV and cousin of Antiochus V, escaped from Rome (where he had gone as a hostage when Antiochus IV had been released), killed both Lysias and Antiochus V, and assumed the throne. He confirmed Alcimus as high priest (162) of Israel and sent him with an army to Judea under his general Bacchides. The Hasidim accepted Alcimus as the high priest probably, it can be conjectured, because he was of Aaronic descent and because the Syrians (or Seleucids) had guaranteed them freedom of worship. Thus the Hasidim broke from Judas's ranks, but they quickly returned when Alcimus, disregarding his promise not to harm them, slew sixty of them (1 Macc. 7:15–20; Josephus Ant. xii.10.2 [393–97]). Hence Alcimus asked Demetrius for more military help against Judas and his followers, called the HASIDEANS (2 Macc. 14:6). Demetrius sent NICANOR, but he was defeated and killed at Adasa (6 km, 4 mi, N of Jerusalem) on 13 Adar (Mar. 9) 161, (which the Jews celebrate annually as Nicanor's Day); the army fled to Gazara (32 km, 20 mi, W of Adasa) and was destroyed. Alcimus fled to Syria (1 Macc. 7:26–50; Josephus Ant. xii.10.3–5 [398–412]).

Judas sent for help from Rome, but before any could arrive, Demetrius sent Bacchides with Alcimus to avenge Nicanor's death. Because of the might of the Syrian army, many deserted Judas, and in the Battle of Elasa (about 16 km, 10 mi, N of Jerusalem) he was slain (160). His brothers Jonathan and Simon took his body to be buried at Modein (1 Macc. 8:1–9:22; Josephus Ant. xii.10.6–11.2 [413–434]).

D. Jonathan (160–143 B.C.) Judas's death was a great blow to morale. The Hellenists were temporarily in control while Jonathan and his followers were in the wilderness of Tekoa, waging only guerrilla warfare. Bacchides fortified Jerusalem and other Judean cities against possible Maccabean attacks. In May, 159 B.C., Alcimus died, and no successor was chosen. Soon after, Bacchides left his command in Judah and returned to Antioch (157); he went back to Jerusalem at the request of the Hellenists but was defeated at Beth-basi (10 km, 6 mi, S of Jerusalem). He made a peace treaty with Jonathan and then returned to Antioch.

This treaty weakened the Hellenists' position. Jonathan made Michmash (14 km, 9 mi, S of Jerusalem) his headquarters, where he judged the people, punishing the hellenizers (1 Macc. 9:23–27; Josephus Ant. xiii.1.1–6 [1–34]). During the next five years his power increased. In 152 he was further helped by internal struggles for power in Syria. A pretender, Alexander Balas, who claimed to be the son of Antiochus Epiphanes, challenged Demetrius I. Both desired Jonathan's support. Fortunately, Jonathan sided with Alexander Balas, for in 150 Demetrius was slain in a battle against Alexander. Alexander made Jonathan a general, governor, and high priest of Judah and considered him one of his chief friends (1 Macc. 10:22–66; Josephus Ant. xiii.2.3f [46–61]; 4.1f [80–85]). This was certainly a strange alliance, i.e., Alexander Balas, professed son of Antiochus Epiphanes, in league with a Maccabean!

New troubles came in Syria. Demetrius's son, Demetrius II Nicator, challenged Alexander Balas in 147 and finally defeated him in 145. Since Demetrius II was only sixteen and inexperienced, Jonathan took the opportunity to attack the Acra in Jerusalem, where the Hellenistic Jews were still in control. Although Demetrius II opposed the attack, he later conceded to Jonathan by confirming his high-priesthood and granting his request for three districts in southern Samaria. Jonathan was not able to conquer the Acra, however.

In 143 Demetrius II's army rebelled, and Diodotus Trypho (a general of Alexander Balas) claimed the Syrian throne (becoming its first non-Seleucid king) in the name of Alexander Balas's son Antiochus VI. Jonathan took advantage of the situation and sided with Trypho, who in turn made him civil and religious head of the Jews and his brother Simon head of the military. Trypho, however, fearful of Jonathan's success, deceived him, arranged a meeting with him, and subsequently killed him. Jonathan was buried at Modein (1 Macc. 10:67–13:30; Josephus Ant. xiii.4.3–6.6 [86–212]).

Jonathan was succeeded by Simon, the only remaining son of Mattathias. A new phase of the Maccabean rule had emerged. Although generally speaking one does apply the term "Hasmonean" to the whole of the Maccabean family, it is more specifically applied to the high-priestly house from the time of Simon to Rome's intervention in 63 because in that period the Maccabean dream had finally come true, namely, the Israelites had become an independent nation. Hence the political and religious life was headed by one family or dynasty—the Hasmoneans.[41]

**Daniel 11:33-35** Updated American Standard Version (UASV)

33 And those having insight among the people will **impart**
**understanding to the many**; yet they will be made to stumble by sword and
by flame, by captivity and by plundering, for some days. **34** Now when they
stumble, they will be given a **little help**; and many will join with them by
means of smooth speech. **35** And some of those having insight will stumble,
in order **to refine, purge and cleanse them** until the time of the end;
because it is still to come at the appointed time.

The Jews who believed and knew the Hebrew Scriptures, "imparted understanding to the many," as they also suffered under severe persecution. The vast majority of the Jews, however, would become apostates, falling away or standing off from the truth, while the few Jews committed to the only true God of the Scriptures would receive "little help" from their fellow brothers. Many of the faithful remnant suffered martyrdom. This persecution of God's true followers would carry over into Christianity, or "the time of the end; because it is still to come at the appointed time," that is until the Second Coming of Christ. "The mention of "the end," however, serves as a transition. From verse 36 on, the prophecy leaps the intervening centuries to predict events related to the last generation prior to God's judgment of Gentile power and its rulers—prophecy that has yet to be fulfilled."[42]

---

41 H. W. Hoehner, "Maccabees," ed. Geoffrey W Bromiley, *The International Standard Bible Encyclopedia*, Revised (Wm. B. Eerdmans, 1979–1988), 198–199.

42 Walvoord, John. *Daniel* (The John Walvoord Prophecy Commentaries) (Kindle Locations 6307-6309). Moody Publishers.

# CHAPTER 4 The Kings of the South and the North - Daniel 11:36-45 (the End Times)

**Daniel 11:36-37** Updated American Standard Version (UASV)

36 "Then the king will **do as he pleases**, and he will exalt and magnify himself above every god and will speak astonishing things against the God of gods; and he will prosper until the indignation is finished, for that which is decreed will be done. 37 He will show no regard for the gods of his fathers or for the desire of women, nor will he show regard for any other god; for he will magnify himself above them all.

Daniel 11:36-37 seems to depict the rule of the Antichrist in a similar vein as the preceding and succeeding verses. This figure is depicted as one who defies religious norms and glorifies himself above all else. As outlined in verse 36, the Antichrist, referred to as "the king," will do as he pleases, exalting himself above all gods. His words against the God of gods could be seen as blasphemous declarations, defying religious norms and conventions in a manner that shocks and astonishes those who hear them. He will prosper until his time is up - this implies that his success is temporary, limited to a certain span of time decided by divine will.

In verse 37, the Antichrist continues his defiance of traditional belief systems by showing no regard for the gods worshipped by his predecessors or for any other god. This could indicate that he is discarding old religious systems, traditions, and beliefs in favor of his own self-glorification. The phrase "the desire of women" could be interpreted in several ways, but one common understanding is that it refers to a prominent deity or object of worship that is desirable or highly respected, implying further disregard for traditionally revered entities. Alternatively, it may suggest a lack of regard for societal norms and relationships, including marriage. Again, the Antichrist magnifies himself above all, embodying arrogance and self-aggrandizement.

These verses, when viewed in the light of the context, reveal that the Antichrist will not only possess substantial military and economic power, but will also elevate himself above all religious institutions and traditional beliefs. This religious rebellion could be part of his strategy to undermine existing societal structures and norms, consolidating more power and control for himself.

Moreover, the king's disregard for the "gods of his fathers" and his elevation of a previously unknown "god of fortresses" in the subsequent verse (Daniel 11:38) might reflect the transition from a traditionally religious society to a militaristic and wealth-driven society, which are key factors contributing to his rise to power.

These verses are, therefore, consistent with the interpretation of the Antichrist as a powerful figure who uses military might, wealth, and religious rebellion to achieve and maintain global dominance. However, the narrative also emphasizes the temporary nature of his rule, which will come to an end in due course. This serves as a potent reminder of the transient nature of earthly power and the ultimate triumph of divine justice.

**Daniel 11:38** Updated American Standard Version (UASV)

38 But instead he will give glory to the god of fortresses; to a god that his fathers did not know he will give glory by means of gold and silver and precious stones and desirable things.

Daniel 11:38 seems to fit well within this interpretation, offering a description of the Antichrist's worship practices. The verse states that the Antichrist "will give glory to the god of fortresses," which could be understood as the Antichrist placing emphasis on military might and warfare as his primary means of achieving dominance. The concept of "the god of fortresses" likely represents an ideology or system that glorifies force and conquest, aligning with the depiction of the Antichrist as a formidable military power.

This verse also notes that the Antichrist will glorify "a god that his fathers did not know." This suggests the Antichrist will espouse a previously unrecognized or unconventional ideology or belief system that deviates from traditional faiths. The phrase might further imply that the Antichrist's beliefs are unique or revolutionary, leading to new methods of controlling and manipulating others.

This belief system or ideology is upheld by the Antichrist "by means of gold and silver and precious stones and desirable things." This phrase could be interpreted as an indication of how the Antichrist uses material wealth and resources to enforce and promote his ideology. The Antichrist might use wealth not only as a tool for control but also as a symbol of his power and dominance. This aligns with the narrative's depiction of the Antichrist as a figure who exercises both military and economic control.

Therefore, Daniel 11:38 is in line with the broader interpretation of the passage. It portrays the Antichrist as a figure who uses a previously unknown ideology or system, symbolized by the "god of fortresses," to achieve global dominance. This ideology is maintained and enforced using wealth and resources, further emphasizing the Antichrist's extensive control in both military and economic spheres. This interpretation harmonizes with the portrayal of the Antichrist's rule in "the time of the end," further fleshing out his strategies for maintaining power and dominance.

**Daniel 11:39** Updated American Standard Version (UASV)

39 He will act effectively against the most fortified strongholds, along with a foreign god; he will give great honor to those who acknowledge him and will cause them to rule over the many, and he will distribute land for a price.

Given this contextual background, Daniel 11:39 can be understood as describing the Antichrist's rule and the methods by which he maintains power. The verse states that he will "act effectively against the most fortified strongholds," suggesting he will successfully attack or conquer the most defensible positions, indicating considerable military might. This aligns with the overarching depiction of the Antichrist as a formidable military force in "the time of the end."

The verse also mentions the Antichrist acting "along with a foreign god," a phrase open to interpretation. In light of the description of the "king of the North" as leading a group of atheistic, Antichrist nations, this foreign god could refer to a previously unknown or unrecognized ideology, system, or belief that the Antichrist leverages to control and manipulate others.

Moreover, the Antichrist "will give great honor to those who acknowledge him." This could indicate a system of rewards or recognitions for loyalty, further solidifying his reign by incentivizing allegiance. This aligns with the depiction of the Antichrist as a shrewd political figure who knows how to manipulate individuals and nations to achieve his ends.

The verse concludes with, "and he will cause them to rule over the many, and he will distribute land for a price." This suggests that the Antichrist will establish a hierarchy where those loyal to him will be given power over others. This creates a system of governance where loyalty is rewarded with power and authority, thereby ensuring the continuation of his rule. The act of distributing land for a price implies a reshaping of geopolitical territories, further emphasizing the Antichrist's dominance and control over global affairs. This might also allude to his economic influence, as he manipulates resources to maintain his power base.

Hence, Daniel 11:39 offers a detailed account of the strategies employed by the Antichrist to establish and maintain his reign. It serves as a sobering reminder of the extent of his dominance during "the time of the end" but within the larger context, the verse also reinforces the temporary nature of this rule, pointing towards his eventual downfall.

**Daniel 11:40** Updated American Standard Version (UASV)

40 "At the time of the end, the king of the south will attack him, but the king of the north will rush upon him like a whirlwind, with chariots and horsemen, and with many ships; and he will come into countries and will overflow and pass through.

Daniel 11:40 outlines the Antichrist's battles, presented in verses 40 to 45. These passages suggest the timeline of these events to be during "the time of the end" (v. 40). There is no contextual restriction on the term 'end,' implying a reference to the conclusion of all existence. Importantly, this conflict culminates in the Antichrist's downfall (v. 45), succeeded by the resurrection of the holy ones (12:2). These occurrences haven't happened yet, hence, the 'end' mentioned must pertain to the closing phase of our current era.

The phrase "chariots and horsemen, and with many ships" is believed to symbolize modern weaponry that would be employed in this prophesied war. The terms "the king of the South" and "the king of the North" which, earlier in this chapter stood for the rulers of Egypt and Syria respectively, are likely to denote nations or groups of nations during the final days.

Given the current geopolitical situation, neither contemporary Egypt nor Syria have the international influence that their ancient counterparts (the Ptolemaic and Seleucid Empires) enjoyed. Therefore, 'North' and 'South' are likely references in relation to Israel: **Egypt** [King of the South/United States and ally nations] **Syria** [King of the North/atheistic, Antichrist nations] Without committing to it entirely because world scene changes rapidly and often in these last days, this author would suggest China as the King of the North at this time.

In the given context, "the king of the North" appears to refer to a group of nations led by the Antichrist, devoid of any religious belief. However, the exact identity of the "king of the South" is assumed to be the United States and any potential allied powers, should they regain their former status.

If the Antichrist is the king of the North, then the southern nation - or the United States and its allies - would need to have a military force substantial enough to contest his supremacy. The conflict between the kings of the north and the south can be seen as a struggle for global dominance.

The narrative suggests that a southern force, referred to as "the king of the South," will instigate an attack on the Antichrist, or "the king of the

North." In response, the Antichrist is expected to counterattack, overpowering his opposition. This is implied by the phrases "against him," referring to the king of the South, and "will invade" the "countries" of those who initiated the attack, taking control over them effortlessly.

**Daniel 11:41** Updated American Standard Version (UASV)

41 And he will come into the beautiful land and many will fall victim, but these will escape from his power: Edom and Moab and the foremost of the sons of Ammon.

Daniel 11:41 continues to describe the Antichrist's military campaign during "the time of the end." Here, the Antichrist is depicted as invading "the beautiful land," which traditionally is taken to mean Israel, given the context of biblical prophecy. This would fit with the earlier interpretation of the 'North' and 'South' as geopolitical entities relative to Israel.

In this conquest, many will fall victim to the Antichrist's power. This is consistent with the earlier assertion that the Antichrist and his allies will have a considerable military force, enabling them to dominate and take control over other nations.

However, the prophecy also states that some regions will escape from the Antichrist's power: Edom, Moab, and the foremost of the sons of Ammon. These regions, in modern-day terms, refer to parts of Jordan and surrounding areas. The reason for their escape is not explicit in this verse. However, it might be due to geographical advantages, strategic insignificance to the Antichrist's plan, or divine intervention.

This verse also aligns with the previous interpretation of the timeline. The events described, including the Antichrist's invasion of Israel and the fall of many victims, have not yet happened, thus further emphasizing that the 'end' mentioned refers to future events, possibly the closing phase of our current era.

The narrative continues to portray a world in which power struggles and warfare are prevalent, reinforcing the depiction of the Antichrist as a major military and political figure during this prophesied period. Meanwhile, the specific mention of places that will escape the Antichrist's power suggests there will be areas of refuge or resistance in this future landscape.

**Daniel 11:42-43** Updated American Standard Version (UASV)

42 And he will stretch out his hand against countries and the land of
Egypt will not escape. 43 And he will rule over the hidden treasures of gold

and silver and over all the desirable things of Egypt; and the Libyans and the Ethiopians will be at his steps.

In verses 42 and 43 of Daniel 11, the prophetic narrative of the Antichrist's military conquests continues to unfold, fitting into the larger framework of "the time of the end" that has been consistently portrayed throughout this passage.

Verse 42 predicts that the Antichrist will extend his power against various countries and that **Egypt** [United States and ally nations] will not escape his reach. This further emphasizes the depiction of the Antichrist as a powerful global figure during this prophesied period. Despite the modern geopolitical status of **Egypt** [United States and ally nations] not aligning with its ancient status as a powerful empire, it seems to retain a symbolic or strategic significance in this eschatological scenario, being specifically named as a nation that the Antichrist will make every effort to conquer.

Verse 43 further illustrates the extent of the Antichrist's dominion, stating that he will rule over Egypt's "hidden treasures of gold and silver and over all the desirable things of Egypt." This could symbolize the Antichrist's total control over the wealth and resources of the nations he conquers. The nature of the Antichrist's rule is thus not only military but also economic.

Additionally, "the Libyans and the Ethiopians will be at his steps" could suggest that these regions (modern-day Libya and Ethiopia) will follow or succumb to the Antichrist's influence or control. However, the phrase "at his steps" might also imply a certain degree of reluctant subservience or enforced alliance rather than willing cooperation.

Taken together, these verses reinforce the idea of the Antichrist as a formidable military and political power during "the time of the end," expanding his dominion over various nations. These verses also indicate that, despite some regions being mentioned as escaping from his power (like Edom, Moab, and parts of Jordan), many other nations will fall under his control, contributing to the global scale of this conflict.

This interpretation remains consistent with the earlier contextual understanding that these events have not yet occurred, and the 'end' referred to in the passage signifies future events, possibly in the final phase of our current era. The narrative continues to portray a world in flux, where power struggles and warfare dominate the landscape during this prophesied period.

**Daniel 11:44-45** Updated American Standard Version (UASV)

**44** But reports out of the east and out of the north will disturb him, and he will go out in a great rage to annihilate and to devote many to destruction. 45 And he shall pitch his palatial tents between the sea and the glorious holy mountain. Yet he shall come to his end, with none to help him.

Daniel 11:44-45 marks the climax of the Antichrist's conquest and, importantly, his downfall, an event that has been prophesied since the early verses of this passage. This culminating sequence resonates with the rest of the narrative's overarching theme of "the time of the end."

In verse 44, reports or tidings from the "east and the north" are said to disturb the Antichrist, leading him to act out "in a great rage to annihilate and to devote many to destruction." The reference to the 'east' and 'north' could suggest threats or challenges arising from those directions, possibly from nations or powers not previously engaged in the conflicts described in the earlier verses. Given the broader interpretation that this passage relates to a future global conflict, the 'east' and 'north' might refer to other major global powers or coalitions that become involved.

It's significant that these reports will "disturb" the Antichrist and incite him to act in "great rage." This could imply a turning point in the conflict, where the Antichrist feels threatened or challenged, leading him to respond with increased violence. This fits the portrayal of the Antichrist as a leader who reacts with force and intimidation when his authority is contested.

Verse 45 describes the Antichrist setting up his "palatial tents between the sea and the glorious holy mountain." Considering the larger biblical context, "the glorious holy mountain" is usually identified with Mount Zion in Jerusalem, Israel. This placement of his headquarters or base suggests a strategic positioning to consolidate his power and perhaps an attempt to assert control over the religious or spiritual heartland represented by Jerusalem. This fits with the earlier interpretation of the 'North' and 'South' as geopolitical entities relative to Israel.

Yet, despite his military and political prowess, verse 45 concludes with the prediction that the Antichrist "shall come to his end, with none to help him." This echoes the broader prophetic narrative in which the Antichrist, despite his apparent power and dominion, ultimately falls. This downfall, left unaided, marks the end of his reign and signals the impending resurrection of the holy ones as mentioned in Daniel 12:2.

These verses, therefore, reaffirm the view that these prophetic events are situated in a future timeline, the "time of the end." They further depict a world characterized by escalating conflicts, increasing turmoil, and a decisive power struggle involving major global entities. However, they also provide a reassuring message: despite the formidable power of the Antichrist, his reign is temporary and doomed to end, making way for divine justice and restoration.

**Who is Gog of the Land of Magog Mentioned by Ezekiel the Prophet?**

**Ezekiel 38:16** Updated American Standard Version (UASV)

16 and **you will come up against my people** Israel like a cloud covering the land; it will be in the last days, and I will bring you against my land, so that the nations know me, when I show myself holy through you before their eyes, O Gog!"

So, who is Gog of the land of Magog? Initially, it would seem that the name "Gog" might have been a proper name that over time came to be used as a general title for an enemy of God's people. However, for us to answer that question, we need to search through the entire Bible and see who attacks God's people in a major way. The Bible mentions the attack by 'Gog of the land of Magog,' the attack by "the king of the north," and the attack by "the kings of the earth." (Ezekiel 38:2, 10-13; Daniel 11:40, 44, 45; Revelation 17:14; 19:19) These may very well be different attacks against God's people (the Israelites Ezekiel 38:2, 10-13), which culminate into the final attack by the enemies of God right after the end of the great tribulation. Jesus Christ at Armageddon saves God's chosen people by destroying Gog of Magog. We know that all of the nations of the earth are enemies of God's people at the time of the final attack at the beginning of the war of Armageddon. (Revelation 16:14, 16) After that, we enter into the literal thousand-year reign of Christ. So, Gog of Magog refers to a composite group of nations at the time of Armageddon that opposes God's people.

Notice what God says about Gog: "You will come from your place out of the remote parts of the **north**, you and many peoples with you, all of them riding on horses, a great assembly and a mighty army." (Ezekiel 38:6, 15) The prophet Daniel who lived at the same time as Ezekiel, had this to say about the king of the north: "But reports out of the east and out of the **north** will disturb him, and he will go out in a great rage to annihilate and to devote many to destruction. And he shall pitch his palatial tents between the sea and the glorious holy mountain. Yet he shall come to his end, with none to help him." (Daniel 11:44-45) Note that this is similar to what the prophet Ezekiel says that Gog will do. – Ezekiel 38:8-12, 16.

What will happen after the final attack of Gog of Magog, the composite nations of the earth, on God's people? Daniel tells us: "Now at that time [at Armageddon] Michael [the archangel, the most powerful angel], the great prince who stands up for the sons of your people, will arise. And there will be a time of distress [the great tribulation] such as never occurred since there was a nation until that time; and at that time your people, everyone who is found written in the book, will be rescued." – Daniel 12:1.

We know that these difficult times for true Christians today will only go from bad to worse. (2 Timothy 3:1-7) However, we have no need to be overly anxious about the coming attacks on God's people. Rather, our focus at present should be on the sanctification of God and to make known his sovereignty to the world. We know that "the Lord knows how to rescue the godly from trials,[43] and to keep the unrighteous under punishment until the day of judgment." (2 Peter 2:9) In the meantime, we want to strengthen our faith so that we may remain steadfast no matter how any future attacks may impact us. We should have a good prayer life, a personal study program, attend Christian meetings faithfully. – Hebrews 6:19; 10:24-25; Psalm 25:21.

While we are on the subject of God of the land of Magog, we might as well address who is Gog **and** Magog of Revelation 20:8. Remember, God of the land of Magog represented the composite nations, who were to attack God's people at the end of the great tribulation that begins Armageddon. Here Gog **and** Magog of Revelation 20:8 seem likely that it is referring to all of the people who will attack God's true people with the same hateful vigor at the end of the thousand-year reign of Christ when Satan is let loose from the abyss. Just as God of Magog, Gog **and** Magog will also be destroyed. – Revelation 19:20, 21; 20:9.

---

[43] Or *temptation*

# CHAPTER 5 The Time of the End - 33 A.D. to the Great Tribulation to Armageddon

**Daniel 12:1** Updated American Standard Version (UASV)

**12** "Now at that time Michael,[44] the great prince who stands up for the sons of your people, will arise. And there will be a time of distress such as never occurred since there was a nation until that time; and at that time your people, everyone who is found written in the book, will be rescued.

**Now, at that time –** refers to in the preceding chapter just described in Daniel 11:36-45. More specifically, the reference is primarily to 11:40, "the time of the end." Revelation can only be fully understood after it *has taken place* or lesser so *as it is taking place*, or even less as *it is beginning to occur*. 'Daniel was to conceal the words and seal up the book until the time of the end; then, many would examine the book thoroughly, and knowledge would increase.

**Michael, the great prince who stands up** – Who is Michael? **Archangel**: (ἀρχάγγελος archaggelos) Michael (מִיכָאֵל Mikael/Μιχαήλ Michaēl) is the only spirit named as an archangel in the Bible. Nevertheless, some Bible scholars believe that 'it is possible that there are other archangels. However, the prefix "arch," meaning "chief" or "principal," indicates that there is only one archangel, the chief angel. Yes, Gabriel is very powerful, but no Scripture ever refers to him as an archangel. If there were multiple archangels, how could they be described as arch (chief or principal) angels? In the Scriptures, "archangel" is never found in the plural. Clearly, Michael is the only archangel, and as the highest-ranking angel, like the highest-ranking general in the army, Michael stands directly under the authority of God, as he commands the other angels, including Gabriel, according to the Father's will and purposes. Michael, the Archangel, whose name means, "Who is like God?"); he disputed with Satan over Moses' body. (Jude 9) Michael with Gabriel stood guard over the sons of Israel and fought for Israel against demons. (Dan. 10:13, 21) He cast Satan and the demons out of heaven. (Rev. 12:7-9) He will defeat the kings of the earth and their armies at Armageddon, and he will be the one given the privilege of abyssing Satan, the archenemy of God. – Revelation 18:1-2; 19:11-21.

**How does Michael, the great prince who stands up?** Michael, the archangel fights for God's sovereignty.

---

[44] Meaning *Who Is Like God?*

The spirit person or creature named Michael is only mentioned by name five times in the Bible. Nevertheless, he is always in the midst of some very serious intense action when he is mentioned. We have Michael in the book of Daniel battling wicked angels. In the Epistle of Jude, Michael is found disputing with Satan. In the book of Revelation, he is waging war with Satan the Devil and his demon army. As was said, Michael is the highest-ranking angel, who is always found in Scripture defending the sovereignty of God, living up to his name, which means "Who Is Like God?"

Michael is so powerful; no enemy could ever defeat him. Revelation states, "war broke out in heaven: Michael and his angels made war with the dragon, and the dragon and its angels waged war." Michael is the leader of an army of God's faithful angels, including Gabriel. Michael is under the command of Jesus Christ himself. – Matt 13:41; 16:27; 24:31; 2 Thess. 1:7; 1 Pet. 3:22; Rev. 19:14-16.

Michael the archangel is spoken of in the following texts:

**Daniel 10:2, 13, 20-21** Updated American Standard Version (UASV)

2 In those days I, Daniel, was mourning for three weeks. 13 The prince
of the kingdom of Persia withstood me twenty-one days, but Michael, one of
the chief princes, came to help me, for I was left there with the kings of
Persia, 20 Then he said, "Do you know why I have come to you? But now I
will return to fight against the prince of Persia, and when I go out, look, the
prince of Greece will come. 21 But I will tell you what is inscribed in the book
of truth, and there is none who contends by my side against these
except Michael, your prince.

Chapter 10 of the book of Daniel precedes the final vision that was given to Daniel, the battles between The Kings of the North and the South.

Thus, Satan the Devil has been using his power through rebel "angels who did not keep to their own domain but deserted their proper dwelling place [in heaven], he has kept in eternal bonds under deep [spiritual] darkness [known as Tartarus (2 Pet.2:4)] for the judgment of the great day." – Jude 1:6.

These rebel angels had the power at one time to materialize in human form, just like the ones that remain faithful to God, as they delivered messages for Him. (Gen. 18:1, 2, 8, 20-22; 19:1-11; Josh. 5:13-15) The "proper dwelling" that Jude speaks of is heaven, to which these angels abandoned, to take on human form, and have relations that were contrary to nature with the "the daughters of man." (Dan. 7:9-10) The Bible intimates that these rebel angels were stripped of their power to take on human form, as you never hear of it taking place again after the flood, only spirit possession after that. These disobedient angels are now "spirits in prison," who had been thrown into "eternal chains under gloomy darkness," which is more of a condition of limited powers, not so much a place, like a maximum-security prison. – 1 Peter 3:19; 2 Peter 2:4; Jude 6.

While there is little doubt that demons are very dangerous, mighty, and very strong, we still need not dread them. After the flood, their power was limited, and God does use the good angels to protect his servants from demons. After the flood, the rebellious angels returned to heaven. They were not permitted back into the faithful angel's intimate, enlightened spirit family with God. Rather, they were cut off from any spiritual wisdom, knowledge, and understanding from God; after that, only a dark outlook for the future. As was mentioned above, these rebel angels were confined to a condition of spiritual darkness known as Tartarus. (2 Pet. 2:4) God restrained them with "eternal bonds under deep [spiritual] darkness." Again, while they no longer have the power or the ability to materialize in human form, they can possess other humans other than God's true servants and control world affairs under the guidance of the god of this age, Satan the Devil. – 2 Corinthians 4:3-4; 11:13-15.

In the prophetic book of Daniel, we find out how "the world-rulers of this darkness, … the wicked spirit forces in the heavenly places," have been exercising control over the world since ancient times. Daniel was deeply concerned about his fellow countrymen who had returned to Jerusalem after seventy years of Babylonian captivity. He prayed on their behalf for three weeks. A good angel was sent to Daniel by God to comfort him but was delayed, so he informed Daniel, saying, "The prince [rebel angel] of the kingdom of Persia withstood me twenty-one days" – Daniel 10:2, 13.

The angel was clearly not referring to the Persian King Cyrus, who at that time found favor in Daniel and the Israelite people. Moreover, no human could ever hold back a powerful angel for three weeks, for we remember it took but one angel to slaughter 185,000 Assyrian mighty warriors in one night. (Isaiah 37:36) Therefore, this opposing 'prince of Persia' could only be a rebel angel of the Devil, in other words, a demon whom Satan gave control over the Persian Empire. Later in the account, the angel of God would state that he would have to fight once against "the prince of Persia" and another demon rebel angel prince, "the prince of Greece." (Dan. 10:20) Truly, there really are invisible "world rulers," demon rebel princes who have been assigned a role in their control of the world under the authority of their prince of darkness himself, Satan the Devil.

On Daniel 10:13, John Walvoord writes, "This prince is not the human king of Persia, but rather the angelic leader of Persia, a fallen angel under the direction of Satan, in contrast to the angelic prince Michael who leads and protects Israel. That the angel described as 'the prince' of Persia is a wicked angel is clear from the fact that his opposition to the angelic messenger to Daniel was given as the reason for the twenty-one-day delay in the answer."[45] Max Anders writes, "Every conservative commentator agrees that this verse and similar references in verses 20–21 indicate that fallen angels, to some extent, control and protect earthly kingdoms. We learn in verse 20 that Greece also had such a 'prince,' and apparently, as we read in 10:13, Michael may be the guardian angel of Israel."[46] This author would go beyond both Walvoord and Anders and say that Michael is the only archangel (chief or principal), over all of the faithful angels and protecting God's faithful servants. Now, let's look at Daniel 12:1 again.

**Daniel 12:1** Updated American Standard Version (UASV)

**12** "Now at that time **[at Armageddon]** Michael **[the archangel, the most powerful angel]**, the great prince who stands up for the sons of your people, will arise. And there will be a time of distress **[the great tribulation]** such as never occurred since there was a nation until that time; and at that time your people, everyone who is found written in the book, will be rescued.

At the time of Daniel "Michael may be the guardian angel of Israel" or (Anders) "Michael who leads and protects Israel" (Walvoord) would be correct but being that, as Jesus said, "Therefore I say to you, the kingdom of God will be taken away from you [Israel] and given to a nation [Israel of God, Christianity] (Gal. 6:15-16), producing the fruit of it." (Matt 21:45) He later went on to say of Israel, "'Jerusalem, Jerusalem, who kills the prophets and stones those who are sent to her! How often I wanted to gather your children together, the way a hen gathers her chicks under her wings, and you were unwilling. Look, your house **[being the chosen people]** is being left to you desolate! For I say to you, from now on you will not see me until you say, 'Blessed is he who comes in the name of the Lord.'" (Matt 23:37-39) The latter words mean that the Jews were no longer God's chosen people and that the Israel of God, Christianity was replacing them, of any of the Jewish people wanted to be one of God's people again, they needed to accept Jesus Christ and convert from the Jewish religion to Christianity, 'coming in the name of Christ.' So, I would agree in a limited way with Anders and Walvoord that Michael served as a protection for Israel, yet it was **ancient** Israel, but

---

[45] Walvoord, John. Daniel (The John Walvoord Prophecy Commentaries) (p. 246). Moody Publishers. Kindle Edition.

[46] Anders, Max. Holman Old Testament Commentary – Daniel (p. 284). B&H Publishing. Kindle Edition.

he now serves as a protection for the "Israel of God" (Gal. 6:16), true Christianity. He is not a guardian angel of individual persons, but he assigns angels to prevent rebel angels from slaughtering true Christians.

**Jude 1:9-10** Updated American Standard Version (UASV)

9 But Michael the archangel, when he disputed with the devil and argued
about the body of Moses, did not dare to bring a judgment against him in
abusive terms, but said, "The Lord rebuke you!" 10 But these men speak evil
of the things which they do not understand; and the things which they know by instinct, like unreasoning animals, by these things they are corrupting themselves.[47] (See Deut. 34:5-6)

David Walls and Max Anders write, "In an interesting peek behind the historical curtain that we do not get in the Old Testament, we learn that Michael was sent to bury the body of Moses when he died atop Mount Nebo (Deut. 34). According to Jewish tradition (supported by this passage), the devil argued with him about it, apparently claiming for himself the right to dispose of Moses' body. (For Jewish sources, see Bauckham, WBC 50, 65–76.) Michael, powerful as he was, **did not dare to bring a slanderous accusation** against the devil but said instead, **The Lord rebuke you!**"[48]

**Revelation 12:7** Updated American Standard Version (UASV)

7 And war broke out in heaven: Michael and his angels made war with the dragon, and the dragon and its angels waged war,

The heavenly sky-drama marches ahead. The woman and her child fade out. **Michael and his angels** fade in; so do the angels of the dragon. John sees a great sky battle, a **war in heaven**. Try and picture this like a *Star Wars* kind of space battle. This portrays in symbols the truth of Ephesians is 6:12: 'For our struggle is not against flesh and blood, but against the rulers, against the authorities, against the powers of this dark world and against the spiritual forces of evil in the heavenly realms.' Many Bible students have puzzled over why Christ is not portrayed as the leader of the good angels. Michael has a secure place in Scripture as the only named archangel, "ruler of angels," which is undoubtedly his role here (Jude 9). Christ as the supreme heavenly warrior is revealed only in chapter 19. As the fourth character in the drama, Michael has a bit part. This is the only verse in all of Revelation in which he appears."[49] With all due respect to Kendell H. Easley, who says

[47] Or *they are destroyed*

[48] David Walls and Max Anders, *I & II Peter, I, II & III John, Jude*, vol. 11, Holman New Testament Commentary (Nashville, TN: Broadman & Holman Publishers, 1999), 263.

[49] Kendell H. Easley, *Revelation*, vol. 12, Holman New Testament Commentary (Nashville, TN: Broadman & Holman Publishers, 1998), 210–211.

"Michael has a bit part," you need not talk despairingly, "bit part," about Michael the archangel to prop up Jesus Christ, as Michael is only one of two angels mentioned in the Bible and he is the head, the chief, the principal angel over all other angels and has been serving Christ as a protector of his people since the rebels in the Garden of Eden were expelled.

**And there will be a time of distress [the great tribulation] such as never occurred since there was a nation until that time –** Jesus Christ, using Michael the archangel to lead the army of angels to execute and bring an end to Satan's wicked age over imperfect humans during the "great tribulation." – Matthew 24:21; Jeremiah 25:33; 2 Thessalonians 1:6-8; Revelation 7:14; 16:14, 16.

**Matthew 24:21-22** Updated American Standard Version (UASV)

[21] For then there will be great tribulation, such as has not been from the beginning of the world until now, no, and never will be. [22] And if those days had not been cut short, no flesh would have been saved: but for the chosen ones sake those days will be cut short.

> But even in judgment, the Lord will display mercy, particularly for the sake of the elect (plural of eklektos, 'select, chosen ones'). These are those who have placed faith in him and followed him as his disciples. The use of the term elect also highlights the Lords sovereign choice as to who these people will be.[50]

We notice that the texts above do not say that all of the chosen ones will be taken before the great tribulation. Instead, it says that the great tribulation will be cut short for their sake. This suggests that some of the chosen ones will still be present on earth during the great tribulation. Some even survive the great tribulation, meaning that they are there afterward.

**Revelation 7:4, 9-10, 14** Updated American Standard Version (UASV)

[4] And I heard the number of the ones who were sealed, **one hundred forty-four thousand** [See note below] sealed from every tribe of the sons of Israel: [9] After this I saw, and look! a great multitude, which no man was able to number, out of all nations and tribes and peoples and tongues, standing before the throne and before the Lamb, dressed in white robes and with palm branches in their hands. [10] and they cry with a great voice, saying, "Salvation to our God who sits on the throne, and to the Lamb." [14] And I said to him, "My lord, you know." And he said to me, "These are the ones **who have**

[50] Stuart K. Weber, *Matthew, vol. 1, Holman New Testament Commentary* (Nashville, TN: Broadman & Holman Publishers, 2000), 401.

**come out of the great tribulation**, and have washed their robes and made them white in the blood of the Lamb.

> **The case for symbolism is exegetically weak.** The principal reason for the view is a predisposition to make the 144,000 into a group representative of the church with which no possible numerical connection exists. No justification can be found for understanding the simple statement of fact in v. 4 as a figure of speech. **It is a definite number [at 7:4] in contrast with the indefinite number of 7:9.** If it is taken symbolically, no number in the book can be taken literally. As God reserved 7,000 in the days of Ahab (1 Kings 19:18; Rom. 11:4), He will reserve 144,000 for Himself during the future Great Tribulation. (Bold mine)[51]

Some of the chosen ones, who had the great tribulation cut short for their sake, are part of the hundred and forty-four thousand of Revelation 7:4. These "chosen ones" are those who have been chosen out of true Christians by God to rule as kings, priests, and judges with Christ for a literal thousand years. The great multitude is other Christians, who are not a part of the chosen ones, which **are <u>not</u>** going to heaven to serve as kings, priests, and judges with Jesus Christ. The good news is that this great multitude of Christians will survive the great tribulation as well. God created the earth to be inhabited, to be filled with perfect humans, who are over the animals, and under the sovereignty of God. (Gen 1:28; 2:8, 15; Ps 104:5; 115:16; Eccl 1:4) Sin did not dissuade God from his plans (Isa. 45:18); hence, he has saved redeemable humankind by Jesus' ransom sacrifice. It seems that the Bible offers two hopes to redeemed humans, (1) a heavenly hope or (2) an earthly hope. It also seems that those with the heavenly hope are limited in number and are going to heaven to rule with Christ as kings, priests, and judges either on the earth or over the earth from heaven. It seems that those with earthly hope are going to receive eternal life here on a paradise earth as originally intended.

> In the O[ld] T[estament] the kingdom of God is usually described in terms of a redeemed earth; this is especially clear in the book of Isaiah, where the final state of the universe is already called new heavens and a new earth (65:17; 66:22) The nature of this renewal was perceived only very dimly by OT authors, but they did express the belief that a humans ultimate destiny is an earthly one. [It is unwise to speak of the written Word of God as if it were of human origin, saying 'OT authors express the belief,' when what

[51] Robert L. Thomas, *Revelation 1-7: An Exegetical Commentary* (Chicago: Moody Publishers, 1992), 474.

was written is the meaning and message of what God wanted to convey by means of the human author. – Edward D. Andrews] This vision is clarified in the N[ew] T[estament]. Jesus speaks of the "renewal" of the world (Matt 19:28), Peter of the restoration of all things (Acts 3:21). Paul writes that the universe will be redeemed by God from its current state of bondage (Rom. 8:18-21). This is confirmed by Peter, who describes the new heavens and the new earth as the Christian's hope (2 Pet. 3:13). Finally, the book of Revelation includes a glorious vision of the end of the present universe and the creation of a new universe, full of righteousness and the presence of God. The vision is confirmed by God in the awesome declaration: "I am making everything new!" (Rev. 21:1-8).

The new heavens and the new earth will be the renewed creation that will fulfill the purpose for which God created the universe. It will be characterized by the complete rule of God and by the full realization of the final goal of redemption: "Now the dwelling of God is with men" (Rev. 21:3).

The fact that the universe will be created anew [Create anew does not mean complete destruction followed by a re-creation, but instead a renewal of the present universe. – Edward D. Andrews] shows that God's goals for humans is not an ethereal and disembodied existence, but a bodily existence on a perfected earth. The scene of the beatific vision is the new earth. The spiritual does not exclude the created order and will be fully realized only within a perfected creation. (Elwell 2001, 828-29)

## EXCURSION: Explaining the Tribulation

### The Abomination of Desolation

**Matthew 24:15** Updated American Standard Version (UASV)

**15** "Therefore when you see the abomination of desolation, which was spoken of through Daniel the prophet, standing in the holy place (let the reader understand),

Matthew 24:13 reads, "But **the one who endures <u>to the end</u>** will be saved." Matthew 24:14 said, "this gospel of the kingdom will be proclaimed throughout the whole world as a testimony to all nations, **and then <u>the end</u> <u>will come</u>**." Matthew 24:15 begins with the Greek word *hotan* "whenever" followed by *oun* "therefore, which reads in English, "Therefore when," which connects what preceded, "**the end**," and leads into what follows. Let us take a moment to investigate verse 15.

In verse 3-14, Jesus outlined the signs of "the end of the age." Here in Mathew 24:15, Jesus begins with, "**Therefore when** you see the abomination of desolation, which was spoken of through Daniel the prophet, standing in the holy place (let the reader understand)." If we look at the corresponding accounts in Mark and Luke, they offer us additional insights. Mark 13:14 says, "standing where it ought not to be." Luke 21:20 adds Jesus' words, "But when you see Jerusalem surrounded by armies, then know[52] that its desolation has come near." The complete picture is an "abomination" "standing in the holy place," i.e., "where it ought not be," namely, "Jerusalem surrounded by armies,"

This refers to the Roman army, which assaulted Jerusalem and its temple starting in 66 C.E., under General Cestus Gallus. The temple was the "holy place," and the abomination was the Roman army "standing where it ought not to be." As for the "desolation," this came in 70 C.E. when General Titus of the Roman army completely desolated Jerusalem and its temple. Specifically, what was this "abomination"? Moreover, in what sense was it "standing in the holy place"?

Jesus had urged the readers to *understand*. What was it that they were to *understand*? They were to *understand* that "which was spoken of through Daniel the prophet," i.e., Daniel 9:27. Part "b" of verse 27 reads, "And upon the wing of abominations shall come the one causing desolation, even until a complete destruction, one that is decreed, is poured out on the one causing desolation." – Daniel 9:26-27; see also Daniel 11:31; 12:11.

> The *abomination of desolation* is an expression that recurs in Daniel with some variation in wording (Daniel 8:13; 9:27; 11:31; 12:11), where most scholars agree that there is a reference to the desecration perpetrated by Antiochus Epiphanes when he built an altar to Zeus in the temple and offered swine and other unclean animals on it as sacrifices (cf. 1 Macc. 1:41–61).[53]

We can have it but one of two ways, as Jesus' words were a clear reference to the Roman armies of 66–70 C.E. It may very well be that Daniel's prophecy points to Antiochus Epiphanes "who in 167 [B.C.E., 200-years before Jesus uttered his prophecy] plundered the temple, ordered the sacrificial system to cease, and polluted the altar of the Lord by turning it into

[52] Or *then recognize*

[53] Leon Morris, *The Gospel According to Matthew*, The Pillar New Testament Commentary (Grand Rapids, MI; Leicester, England: W.B. Eerdmans; Inter-Varsity Press, 1992), 603.

a pagan altar, where unclean sacrifices were offered to pagan deities."[54] This would be no different from Matthew referring to Hosea 11:1 (When Israel was a child … and out of Egypt I called my son). In that case, Matthew did not use Hosea's intended meaning but carried out an *Inspired Sensus Plenior Application*, by having a whole other meaning, an entirely different meaning for those words, making them applicable to Jesus being called back out of Egypt. It could be that Jesus used Daniel's prophecy about Antiochus Epiphanes, and gave is an *Inspired Sensus Plenior Application*, by having a whole other meaning, a completely different meaning for those words, making them applicable to the Roman armies desolating Jerusalem between 66 and 70 C.E. Then, again, it could be that was what Daniel was pointing to all along, and Jesus used Daniel's words in a grammatical-historical application. Either way, it still comes out the same.

> During the days of the Maccabees this expression was used to describe the sacrilege of Antiochus IV Epiphanes, the Seleucid king who decreed that an altar to Olympian Zeus and perhaps a statue of himself were to be erected in the temple on 15 Chislev, 167 b.c.: "They erected a desolating sacrilege on the altar of burnt offering. They also built altars in the surrounding towns of Judah." Antiochus further decreed that the Sabbath and other festal observances were to be profaned, that circumcision was to be abolished, and that swine and other unclean animals were to be sacrificed in the temple (cf. 1 Macc. 1:41–50). This was one of the lowest points of Jewish history and was considered by many the primary focus of Daniel's prophecy. Jesus now quotes Daniel directly to clarify that the fulfillment of the "abomination that causes desolation" is yet future.[55]

When Jesus uttered those words of verse 15, the abomination of desolation was yet to appear. Jesus was clearly pointing to the Roman army of 66 C.E., with its distinctive standards, idols to the Romans and the empire, but an abomination to the Jews.

---

[54] Larry Chouinard, *Matthew*, The College Press NIV Commentary (Joplin, MO: College Press, 1997), Mt 24:15.

[55] Clinton E. Arnold, *Zondervan Illustrated Bible Backgrounds Commentary: Matthew, Mark, Luke*, vol. 1 (Grand Rapids, MI: Zondervan, 2002), 148.

Judæa was under the charge of a Roman official, a subordinate of the governor of the Roman province of Syria. He held a relation to that functionary similar to that which the Governor of Bombay holds to the Governor-General at Calcutta. Roman soldiers paraded the streets of Jerusalem; **Roman standards** waved over the fastnesses of the country; Roman tax-gatherers sat at the gate of every town. To the Sanhedrin, the supreme Jewish organ of government, only a shadow of power was still conceded, its presidents, the high priests, being mere puppets of Rome, set up and put down with the utmost caprice. So low had the proud nation fallen whose idea it had ever been to rule the world and whose patriotism was a religious and national passion as intense and unquenchable as ever burned in any country.[56]

*STANDARD OF THE 10TH ROMAN LEGION This Legion attacked and destroyed Jerusalem in the Jewish War (A.D. 70).*

| **Matthew 24:16** (UASV) | **Mark 3:14b** (UASV) | **Luke 21:21** (UASV) |
|---|---|---|
| 16 then let those who are in Judea flee to the mountains. | 14 "… then let those who are in Judea flee to the mountains. | 21 Then let those who are in Judea flee to the mountains, and let those who are in the midst of the city depart, and let not those who are out in the country enter it; |

Looking at verse 20 of Luke 21, we know that it fits the fact that General Cestius Gallus had "the holy city" Jerusalem (Matt. 4:5)[57] surrounded, which

[56] James Stalker, *The Life of Jesus Christ* (Chicago: Henry A. Sumner and Company, 1882), 30–31.

[57] **Matthew 4:5** English Standard Version (ESV)

5 Then the devil took him to the holy city and set him on the pinnacle of the temple

had become the center of the Jewish revolt against Rome. Thirty-three years had passed since Jesus uttered his prophecy, but now the "abomination of desolation" of Rome was near. Gallus and his armies were responding to the Jewish revolt at the celebration of the festival of booths (tabernacles), October 19-25. On about November 3-4, the Roman army entered the city of Jerusalem, where they attacked the temple wall for five days, weakening it on the sixth day. However, for some unforsaken reason, he pulls away. On this attack of Cestius Gallus, Josephus' *Wars of the Jews 2.539*, says that "had he but continued the siege a little longer, had certainly taken the city; but it was, I suppose, owing to the aversion God had already at the city and the sanctuary, that he was hindered from putting an end to the war that very day." A footnote in Flavius Josephus and William Whiston reads,

> There may another very important, and very providential, reason be here assigned for this strange and foolish retreat of Cestius; which, if Josephus had been now a Christian, he might probably have taken notice of also; and that is, the affording the Jewish Christians in the city an opportunity of calling to mind the prediction and caution given them by Christ about thirty-three years and a half before, that "when they should see the abomination of desolation" [the idolatrous Roman armies, with the images of their idols in their ensigns, ready to lay Jerusalem desolate,] "stand where it ought not;" or, "in the holy place;" or, "when they should see Jerusalem encompassed with armies," they should then "flee to the mountains."
>
> By complying with which those Jewish Christians fled to the mountains of Perea, and escaped this destruction. See Lit. Accompl. of Proph. pp. 69–70. Nor was there, perhaps, any one instance of a more unpolitic, but more providential conduct than this retreat of Cestius, visible during this whole siege of Jerusalem; which yet was providentially such a "great tribulation, as had not been from the beginning of the world to that time; no, nor ever should be."—Ibid., pp. 70–71.[58]

| **Matthew 24:17-18** (UASV) | **Mark 13:15-16** (UASV) |
|---|---|
| [17] Let the man who is on the housetop not go down to take what is in his house, [18] and let the man who is in the field not turn back to take his cloak. | [15] let the man who is on the housetop not go down, nor enter his house, to take anything out; [16] and let the man who is in the field not turn back to take his cloak. |

[58] Flavius Josephus and William Whiston, *The Works of Josephus: Complete and Unabridged* (Peabody: Hendrickson, 1987).

When General Gallus suddenly withdrew his armies for no seemingly good reason, they suffered substantial fatalities at the hands of the Jews, who were pursuing them. This would wake the Jewish and Gentile Christians to Jesus' words and that a great tribulation would soon be upon them. (Matt. 24:21) This allowed them to flee, and for no Christian, to return until the tribulation had passed. Eusebius of Caesarea (260/265 – 339/340 C.E.), a Christian, who was a Roman historian, writes,

> But the people of the church in Jerusalem had been commanded by a revelation, vouchsafed [promised] to approved men there before the war, to leave the city and to dwell in a certain town of Perea called Pella.[59] And when those that believed in Christ had come thither from Jerusalem, then, as if the royal city of the Jews and the whole land of Judea were entirely destitute of holy men, the judgment of God at length overtook those who had committed such outrages against Christ and his apostles, and totally destroyed that generation of impious men. (Eusebius, Ecclesiastical History 3.5.3)

Josephus, the first-century Jewish historian (33–100 C.E.), tells us that the Jews waited for God's help, not realizing this was the day of the Lord, a judgment day upon them,

> A false prophet[60] was the occasion of these people's destruction, who had made a public proclamation in the city that very day, that God commanded them to get up upon the temple, and that there they should receive miraculous signs of their deliverance. Now, there was then a great number of false prophets suborned by the tyrants to impose upon the people, who denounced this to them, that they should wait for deliverance from God: and this was in order to keep them from deserting, and that they might be buoyed up above fear and care by such hopes. Now, a man that is in adversity does easily comply with such promises; for when a such a seducer makes him believe that he shall be delivered from those miseries which oppress him, then it is that the patient is full of hopes of such deliverance. (Josephus, Wars of the Jews 6.285–87)

[59] Pella was a town situated beyond the Jordan, in the north of Perea, within the dominions of Herod Agrippa II. The surrounding population was chiefly Gentile. See Pliny V. I8, and Josephus, B. J. III. 3. 3, and I. 4. 8. Epiphanius (De pond. et mens. 15) also records this flight of the Christians to Pella.

[60] Reland here justly takes notice that these Jews who had despised the true Prophet, were deservedly abused and deluded by these false ones.

Dio Chrysostom expresses wonder at the level of Jewish fight that they possessed to the very end of the revolt,

> The Jews resisted [Titus] with more ardor than ever, as if it were a kind of windfall [an unexpected piece of luck] to fall fighting against a foe far outnumbering them; they were not overcome until a part of the Temple had caught fire. Then some impaled themselves voluntarily on the swords of the Romans, others slew each other, others did away with themselves or leaped into the flames. They all believed, especially the last, that it was not a disaster but victory, salvation, and happiness to perish together with the Temple. (Dio Chrysostom, Orations 66.6–2–3.)

*Zondervan's Illustrated Bible Background Commentary* on Matthew 24:17 tells us, "Likewise, there will not be time to gather provisions in the home. The flat rooftops on many homes in Israel were places to find a cool breeze in the evening and were considered part of the living quarters."[61] In Jewish homes of those who could afford a multiform house, there was a staircase outside that led to the roof. The poor would have had a ladder in the courtyard, which led to the roof. Therefore, anyone on the housetop of their home, which was very common, could leave without having to enter their home. Moreover, many homes were built side-by-side, and it was possible to walk from one rooftop to the next. These backgrounds fit what Jesus meant by the words that he used. Whether Jesus meant his words in a hyperbolic sense of, 'when you see these things, act immediate, do not delay,' or literally, 'do not even look back, get out,' it is clear that Christians considered Jesus' warning serious, knowing that mere materials were not worth the loss of their lives.

*Zondervan's Illustrated Bible Background Commentary* on Matthew comments on verse 18 that "The outer coat was an essential garment for traveling, often used as a blanket when sleeping outdoors, and only those in the greatest hurry would think of leaving it behind."[62] ZIBBC comments on Mark 13:18, saying, "Winter is the time of heavy rains in Palestine, flooding roads and wadis. Gadarene refugees during the first revolt sought shelter in Jericho but could not cross the swollen Jordan and were slain by the Romans. Winter travel is also hazardous if people are to traverse mountain passes." (Arnold 2002, 283)

---

[61] Clinton E. Arnold, *Zondervan Illustrated Bible Backgrounds Commentary: Matthew, Mark, Luke*, vol. 1 (Grand Rapids, MI: Zondervan, 2002), 149.

[62] Clinton E. Arnold, *Zondervan Illustrated Bible Backgrounds Commentary: Matthew, Mark, Luke*, vol. 1 (Grand Rapids, MI: Zondervan, 2002), 149.

**Matthew 24:19** Updated American Standard Version (UASV)

[19] But woe to those who are pregnant and to those who are nursing babies in those days![63]

Indeed, the modern-day woman has taken on some very rigorous activities. Recently, this author saw news of a woman in her eighth month of pregnancy, running a marathon. However, in the days of the first century C.E., an extended flight over mountainous terrain on foot would be arduous and quite dangerous. This would be especially true for any woman close to her due date. When the Romans finally desolated Jerusalem in 70 C.E., pregnant women, and those with young, were shown no mercy by the Roman troops. As the months of laying siege to the city, drug on feminine prevailed, which for a pregnant woman, the baby would be robbing the woman of nourishment. For example, the baby would take the mother's calcium for bone development, meaning the woman could lose all of her teeth. Moreover, some mothers gave birth and had to watch their child starve to death, and in some cases, the people would take the child, cook it and eat it.

**Matthew 24:20** Updated American Standard Version (UASV)

[20] But pray that your flight will not be in the winter, or on a Sabbath.

This verse is self-explanatory, as we can only imagine the Christians trying to escape over mountainous terrain during the winter. Imagine if they ignored the warning, procrastinated until the Roman troops arrived, and had to make their escape in the winter; when, they could have left earlier. *Zondervan's Illustrated Bible Background Commentary* on Matthew comments on verse 18, saying, "Flight in winter, when roads are washed out and rivers are swollen, presents, even more difficulty for those fleeing the horrors of the coming desolation. In prayer the disciples must cling to God's presence and ever-ready help, even though they may have to disrupt even the most devoutly held religious traditions, such as the Jewish Sabbath." (Arnold 2002, 150)

**Matthew 24:21** Updated American Standard Version (UASV)

[21] For then there will be great tribulation, such as has not been from the beginning of the world until now, no, and never will be.

---

[63] In this connection it should be borne in mind that this tender concern for women with babies was revealed by Christ in days when women were often looked down upon. The words uttered came from the lips of the same Son of man who showed special kindness to widows (Mark 12:42, 43; Luke 7:11–17; 18:1–8; 20:47; 21:2, 3); to women who were, or had been, living in sin (Luke 7:36–50; John 4:1–30); and, at the time of his own crowning agony, to his own mother (John 19:26, 27). (Hendriksen and Kistemaker 1953–2001, p. 859)

As we look at Matthew 24:15-22 with Luke 21:20-24, the great tribulation of Jesus' prophecy applies to what took place in Jerusalem. The fulfillment of these words came in 70 C.E., when General Titus and his Roman armies laid siege to the city, desolating it, killing 1,100,000 Jews, whereas 97,000 who survived were taken into captivity. (Whiston 1987, Wars of the Jews 6.420) Some might argue that the 6,000,000 million Jews killed by Hitler during World War II was certainly a greater tribulation than 70 C.E. However, the difference is God used the Roman army as a tool to judge ("a day of the Lord") the Jews for their 1,500 years of false worship, child sacrifice, murder, and the execution of the Son of God. After 70 C.E., Jerusalem was never again the holy city it once was, nor were the Jews God's chosen people. Therefore, the suffering that the Jews faced during World War II was not as a judgment of God, but rather an unexpected or unforeseen event of human imperfection resulting from Adamic sin, no different from any other atrocity on humanity.

**Matthew 24:22** Updated American Standard Version (UASV)

**22** And if those days had not been cut short, no flesh would have been saved: but for the chosen ones[64] sake those days shall be shortened.

Again, these words apply to a preliminary fulfillment in 66-70 C.E. If we recall, the city was under siege by General Cestius Gallus, who had the city surrounded and was undermining the Temple wall. Many of the Jews were ready to surrender, but for some unknown reason, he pulled away, suffering significant casualties at the hands of the pursuing Jews. Had Gallus not pulled away, leaving several years before Titus would come back and finish the job, the chosen ones,[65] i.e., predominantly Jewish and some Gentile Christians, would have not been saved from the desolation. Yes, they heeded Jesus words, "But when you see Jerusalem surrounded by armies, then know[66] that its desolation has come near. Then let those who are in Judea flee to the mountains and let those who are in the midst of the city depart, and let not those who are out in the country enter it." (Luke 21:20-21) Thus, the Christians fled the city that was doomed to suffer the destruction of 70 C.E.

**Matthew 24:23-26** Updated American Standard Version (UASV)

**23** Then if any man says to you, 'Look, here is the Christ!' or 'There he is!' do not believe it. **24** For false Christs and false prophets will arise and will

---

[64] Or *the elect*

[65] These "chosen ones" are those who have been **chosen** out of true Christians by God to rule as kings, priests, and judges with Christ for a literal thousand years.

[66] Or *then recognize*

show great signs and wonders, so as to mislead, if possible, even the chosen ones.[67] **25** Behold, I have told you in advance. **26** So if they say to you, 'Behold, he is in the wilderness,' do not go out, or, 'Behold, he is in the inner rooms,' do not believe it.

We have discussed this aspect extensively earlier. Jesus' prophecy about the end of the Jewish age and the end of wicked humanity reads, "See that no one leads you astray. For many will come in my name, saying, 'I am the Christ,' and they will **lead many <u>astray</u>**." (Matt 24:4-5) Here in our current verses, Jesus tells us who specifically is being "led astray," "For false Christs [Gr., *pseudochristoi*] and false prophets will arise and will show great signs and wonders, so as to mislead, if possible, even **<u>the chosen ones</u>**." Any who falsely claim to be Christ (anointed one or Messiah), or claim to be a special representative of Christ, are included in the "antichrist" [Gr., *antichristos*], which is mentioned five times by the apostle John. (1 John 2:18, 22; 4:3; 2 John 1:7) For more information on the Antichrist, see APPENDIX C.

There were false Christs and false prophets that came on the scene before 70 C.E. and the destruction of the Jewish age. Jewish historian Flavius Josephus confirms this as he writes that before the Romans ever attacked, false Messiahs prompted rebellion. To mention just a couple, there is Menahem ben Judah, who claimed to be the Jewish Messiah and is mentioned by Josephus. Then, there is Theudas, who claimed to be the Messiah, a Jewish rebel of the 1st century C.E., who, between 44 and 46 CE, led his followers in a short-lived revolt. However, as is self-evident, they showed themselves to be false charlatans, as they did not deliver the Jewish people from the Roman armies. After the destruction of Jerusalem, up unto this day, the Jews[68] have put faith in Jesus Christ, the Son of God, but have rather continued their search for a Messiah in the flesh.

Conversely, Jewish and non-Jewish Christians have evidenced their faith in Jesus Christ, as they have continued to look at the end of Satan's rule over the earth, the end of wicked humankind, the return of Jesus Christ and his millennial reign. Many notable people in the 18th to the 21st century have claimed to be the reincarnation or incarnation of Jesus or the Second Coming of Christ. Either they have made these claims, or their followers have made a claim. To mention just a couple, Jim Jones (1931–1978), founder of Peoples Temple, started as a branch of a mainstream Protestant group before becoming a cult. Then, we have Marshall Applewhite (1931–1997), an American, who posted a famous message declaring, "I, Jesus, Son of God,"

---

[67] Or *the elect*

[68] This is not to say that no individual Jewish persons have not converted to Christianity, as hundreds of thousands have in the last two millennium.

whose Heaven's Gate cult committed mass suicide on March 26, 1997. Wayne Bent (1941–), AKA Michael Travesser of the Lord Our Righteousness Church. He claimed, "I am the embodiment of God. I am divinity and humanity combined."

If any reader does not believe that they can fall victim to charismatic persons, they are deceiving themselves. Millions of Christians have fallen victim to such ones, and they have not even had the satanic power of 'showing great signs and wonders,' which will be the result before humanity's "great tribulation." Then, we have Christians that pick up these end-times books, going around speaking of how much truth are within them when the author(s) has gone beyond what the Word of God says. Finally, Pentecostals and Charismatic Christians number over 500 million, a quarter of the world's two billion Christians. This author sees the religious leaders of these groups as the false Christs, antichrists, false prophets that will be the catalyst to the major false Christs, antichrists, false prophets before the great tribulation. **Excessive** emotionalism within Christianity brings about a blind desire for the return of Christ, opening many up to a situation in which religious leaders offer biblical passages that incorrectly match a return of Christ, e.g., signs of the times, a charismatic person, world events, bad prooftexting, and the like.

The information herein is based on the disciples coming to Jesus privately, saying, "Tell us, **(1)** when will these things be, and **(2)** what will be the sign of your coming, and **(3)** of the end of the age?" (Matthew 24:3)

These questions refer to the end of an age, which was referred to in Matthew 24:1-2,

> **1** Jesus came out from the temple and was going away when[69] his disciples came up to point out the temple buildings to him. **2** And he said to them, "Do you not see all these things? **[**the temple buildings**]** Truly I say to you, not one stone here will be left upon another, which will not be torn down."

Jesus refers to the end of the Jewish age, which was to come in 66-70 C.E., with the desolation and destruction of Jerusalem and its temple. The disciples' questions were based on a presumption the end of the temple equal the end of the age, encompassing Christ's return, the judgment of the wicked, and the setting up of his kingdom. The rest of Matthew 24 and 25 is Jesus answering their question. In his words, he addresses what will lead up to the end of the Jewish age, the end of wicked humankind age, and his second coming, his kingdom, and his thousand-year reign. We have to understand

---

[69] Lit *and*

the end of the Jewish age as well because all prophecy has an application to those who hear it, which will help us understand how it applies to the end of sinful, wicked humanity and Christ's return.

**Matthew 24:27-28** Updated American Standard Version (UASV)

27 For just as the lightning comes from the east and flashes even to the west, so will be the coming of the Son of Man. **28** Wherever the corpse is, there the vultures will gather.

The phrase "for just as" helps us appreciate in what sense we should expect the arrival of the Son of Man. Again, without coming across as dogmatic, we will adopt a wait-and-see attitude, but this author does not hold the position that Jesus is coming back here to the earth, but that instead he and his kingdom of co-rulers will be ruling over the earth from heaven. However, just as you can see lightning coming from the east, and vultures from a great distance circling over a corpse, there will be no doubt in the minds of Christians who have stayed awake, remained on the watch, of "the coming of the Son of Man," in that he is ruling under the new millennial reign.

## END OF EXCURSION

**and at that time your people, everyone who is found written in the book, will be rescued –** (See Luke 21:34-36.) What is the book? In essence, it represents those delivered whose names are written in the book of life (Exod. 32:32-33; Ps. 69:28; Rev. 13:8; 17:8; 20:15; 21:27; See also Mal 3:16; Heb. 6:10). Those who have their names inscribed in the book of life have the protection of Michael the archangel, who will use his army of angels, under the direction of Jesus Christ, the King, to rescue them during the great tribulation and Armageddon. And who have lost their lives in past times and any who would lose their lives during the great tribulation and Armageddon **will receive a resurrection**. Acts 24:15; Revelation 20:4-6.

**Daniel 12:2** Updated American Standard Version (UASV)

2 And many of those who sleep in the dust of the earth shall awake, some to everlasting life, and some to shame and everlasting contempt.

Concerning this verse, Stephen R. Miller writes, "In this verse is one of the most astounding and blessed truths in Scripture—the resurrection. After the "time of distress" described in the previous verses, 'multitudes' (*rabbîm*) will be raised from the grave. The resurrected ones are called those 'who sleep in the dust of the earth.' 'Sleep' is a figure of speech used frequently in the Bible to designate physical death (cf. John 11:11–14; Acts 7:60; 1 Thess 4:13;

1 Cor 15:51), and this 'sleep' refers to physical death *only*.[70] Many have no idea that death and sleep are equated because they do not use a good literal translation.

The Hebrew Old Testament and the Greek New Testament render the original language words as "sleep" and "fall asleep," which refer to a sleeping body and a dead body. Below, we can see from the context of Matthew 28:13 that this is physical sleep.

**Matthew 28:13** Updated American Standard Version (UASV)

**κοιμωμένων koimōmenōn**

**Lexical**: sleep; fall asleep

**Literal Translation**: asleep

**Sense**: to be or become asleep

**Matthew 28:13** Updated American Standard Version

13 and said, "Say, 'His disciples came by night and stole him away while we were **asleep**.'

However, in the verses below, the context are to be asleep in death. The figurative extension of the physical sleep in the sense of being at rest and peace. The person in the sleep of death exists in God's memory as they sleep in death; it is only temporary for those who are physically asleep, so it will be true for those sleeping in death.

**Acts 7:60** Updated American Standard Version (UASV)

**ἐκοιμήθη ekoimēthē**

**Lexical**: sleep; fall asleep

**Literal Translation**: asleep

**Sense**: to be asleep in death; the figurative extension of the physical sleep in the sense of being at rest and at peace; the person in the sleep of death exists in God's memory as they sleep in death; it is only temporary for those who are physically asleep, so it will be true of those who are asleep in death.

**Acts 7:60** Updated American Standard Version (UASV)

60 Then falling on his knees, he cried out with a loud voice, "Lord, do not hold this sin against them!" Having said this, he fell **asleep in death**.

---

[70] Stephen R. Miller, *Daniel*, vol. 18, The New American Commentary (Nashville: Broadman & Holman Publishers, 1994), 316.

1 Corinthians 7:39 (UASV)

**κοιμηθῇ koimēthē**

**Lexical**: sleep; fall asleep

**Literal Translation**: asleep

**Sense**: to be asleep in death; the figurative extension of the physical sleep in the sense of being at rest and at peace; the person in the sleep of death exists in God's memory as they sleep in death; it is only temporary for those who are physically asleep, so it will be true of those who are asleep in death.

**1 Corinthians 7:39** Updated American Standard Version (UASV)

39 A wife is bound to her husband as long as he lives. But if her husband falls **asleep in death**, she is free to be married to whom she wishes, only in the Lord.

**1 Thessalonians 4:13** Updated American Standard Version (UASV)

**κοιμωμένων koimaōmenōn**

**Lexical**: sleep; fall asleep

**Literal Translation**: asleep

**Sense**: to be asleep in death; the figurative extension of the physical sleep in the sense of being at rest and at peace; the person in the sleep of death exists in God's memory as they sleep in death; it is only temporary for those who are physically asleep, so it will be true of those who are asleep in death.

**1 Thessalonians 4:13** Updated American Standard Version (UASV)

13 But we do not want you to be ignorant, brothers, about those who are **sleeping in death**, so that you will not grieve as do the rest who have no hope.

Here Paul is addressing the issue of those "who are sleeping" in death (*koimaōmenōn*). *Koimaō* is a common word for sleep that can be used as "to sleep," "sleep," or "fall asleep." However, it is also used in Greek, Jewish, Christian writings and the apostle Paul's letters as a figurative extension of the physical sleep in the sense of being asleep in death. Paul is not using the common sense of the word here, but instead, he is using it to refer to the condition of the dead between death and the resurrection.

**Psalm 13:3** Updated American Standard Version (UASV)

**פֶּן־אִישַׁן הַמָּוֶת׃ pen-išān**

**Lexical**: lest I sleep the death

**Literal Translation**: lest I sleep in death

**Sense**: to be asleep in death; the figurative extension of the physical sleep in the sense of being at rest and at peace; the person in the sleep of death exists in God's memory as they sleep in death; it is only temporary for those who are physically asleep, so it will be true of those who are asleep in death.

**Psalm 13:3** Updated American Standard Version (UASV)

3 Consider and answer me, Jehovah my God;
give light to my eyes
lest I **sleep in death**,

1 Kings 2:10 (UASV)

**שָׁכַב šāḵăḇ**

**Lexical**: lie down; rest; sleep

**Literal Translation**: slept

**Sense**: to be asleep in death; the figurative extension of the physical sleep in the sense of being at rest and at peace; the person in the sleep of death exists in God's memory as they sleep in death; it is only temporary for those who are physically asleep, so it will be true of those who are asleep in death.

**1 Kings 2:10** Updated American Standard Version (UASV)

10 Then David **slept in death** with his forefathers and was buried in the city of David.

Some have argued that the dynamic equivalent thought-for-thought translations (Then David **died** and was buried, NLT) convey the idea in a more clear and immediate way, but is this really the case? Retaining the literal rendering, the metaphorical use of the word sleep is best because of the similarities that exist between physical sleep and the sleep of death. Without the literal rendering, this would be lost on the reader. Retaining the literal rendering, "slept," and adding the phrase "in death" completes the sense in the English text.

We are told by the apostle Paul of those, "having a hope in God, which hope these men await, that there is going to be a resurrection of both the righteous and the unrighteous." (Acts 24:15) This is clear that there is a coming judgment. The apostle Paul understood this, as his next words make clear, "For this reason also I myself always strive to maintain a clear conscience before God and men." (Acts 24:16) Who are the righteous and the unrighteous?

Judgment day is a specific "day" (hardly ever a literal 24 hour day) when certain groups, nations, or humankind are held accountable by God. Jesus said, "The one who rejects me and does not receive my words has a judge; the word that I have spoken will judge him on the last day." (John 12:48) Let's look at Revelation 11:17-18. We see that God begins his judging the moment that he begins ruling in a particular way, i.e., after Armageddon, Jesus' kingdom of co-rulers over the earth for a millennium, the judgment day. During that thousand years reign, the elect, chosen ones, holy ones will serve as judges, priests, and rulers with Christ. In other words, the great multitude who survive Armageddon, the righteous and unrighteous who are resurrected, will be judged throughout the millennium. A thousand-year period can be viewed as a "day," for it is stated in the Bible. (2 Peter 3:8; Psalm 90:4) There is no resurrection from the second death. As we just mentioned, the elect, chosen ones, holy ones who are serving in heaven with Christ as part of his kingdom, are spirit persons and have received immortality, deathlessness, so those who are part of the first resurrection, the second death has no power. The wicked are destroyed at Armageddon, to never be resurrected again, so, neither second death nor judgment day is applicable to them. Jesus promised the elect, "The one who conquers will not be hurt by the second death." The second death has no authority over these ones because they cannot die and have been declared righteous. They will they "will be priests of God and of Christ and will reign with him for a thousand years," judging those on earth. The resurrection and the millennium will be revisited extensively in APPENDIX A.

**Daniel 12:3** Updated American Standard Version (UASV)

3 And the ones who are wise will shine brightly like the brightness of the expanse of heaven; and those who turn many to righteousness, like the stars forever and ever.

**And the ones who are wise –** This expression in the Scriptures is used to indicate those who possess the quality of Godly devotion, who serve God faithfully and love and obey his Word. Allusions or references to this type of language can be found throughout the book of Proverbs. True Christians make up those who are wise, as they who live for God. These wise ones have chosen the path have steadfastly walked with God throughout the latter part of the last days and the Great Tribulation. The language used here is expressive of the righteous.

**will shine brightly like the brightness of the expanse of heaven –** The image we are given is the beauty of the night sky filled with bright and dazzling stars. There is nothing else that could be so appropriately compared that would be so memorable. Each of the righteous ones will be like a bright and beautiful star, and that, when taken as a whole, they would echo the heavenly body of stars at night. There is nothing more majestic, awe-inspiring, and breath-taking than to look on at the heavens on a clear night. Now, ponder that vast body of stars above us as an image of the righteous ones in the latter part of the last days, through the great tribulation and Armageddon, and into a renewed heavenly world. What will these righteous ones be doing during that time leading up to the renewed world?

**those who turn many to righteousness –** This is referring to the righteous ones and that they would be converting "many to righteousness,' that is, to the worship of the true God. This is not referring to those who superficially go to church regularly, even if it is consistent. These righteous ones study for the church meeting they go to each week, have their own personal study and participate in the Bible study group at church. These righteous ones share their faith purposely and even incidentally whenever the opportunity presents itself. They realize that deeper Bible study might not bring an untold number of persons to Christ, but a lack thereof will bring no unbelievers to Christ. These righteous ones are instrumental in turning many to righteousness, to God. – Matthew 24:14; 28:19; Acts 1:8.

**Daniel 12:4** Updated American Standard Version (UASV)

4 But as for you, O Daniel, conceal these words and seal up the book until the time of the end; many shall run to and fro,[71] and knowledge[72] will increase."

What Daniel wrote was concealed and sealed up so that humans really could not understand it. Even Daniel himself could not fully understand his own book, as he stated, "I heard, but I did not understand." (Daniel 12:8) Much of Daniel was understood enough to offer hope to the Israelite people. In this concealing, the Book of Daniel continued sealed for over 2,500 years. What about us today? We are told, "the time of the end; many shall run to and fro," that is, many would examine the book of Daniel thoroughly, which has been the case from the 1800s up until today. What has been the result? It is, as Daniel said, 'knowledge has increased.' As should be expected, hundreds of world-renowned Bible scholars over the past 200+ years have increased the knowledge and meaning of the book of Daniel exponentially.

**Daniel 12:5-6** Updated American Standard Version (UASV)

5 Then I, Daniel, looked and look, two others were standing, one on this bank of the stream and the other on that bank of the stream. 6 And one said

[71] That is, *examine the book thoroughly*

[72] **LXX** "unrighteousness"

to the man clothed in linen, who was above the waters of the stream, "How long shall it be to the end of these wonders?"

Daniel had been fixated on the angel that was disclosing the future events to him. Here Daniel now sees two angelic creatures, unseen before this moment, on the river Hiddekel, also known as the Tigris (cf. 10:4). They had been present this entire time, listening intently about the future events that were just disclosed to Daniel. The angels are deeply interested in knowing the words concealed and sealed up in the book until the time of the end, "into which angels long to look," states the apostle Peter. (1 Pet. 1:12) "The man clothed in linen" was an angel, as when angels have appeared here on earth, they have generally taken on the human form. The name of this angelic creature is not given, but it was likely the same angel who had appeared to him on the banks of the Ulai (Dan. 8:16), and the same angel, Gabriel, who had given him the revelation of the seventy weeks (Dan. 9:21). The question one of these angels raised here to the one given the ability to reveal the future events should interest us all, "How long shall it be to the end of these wonders?" This question of how long had not been addressed up to this point, only events that would go long into the future, but how long no one knew, including the angels. Thus, it was only natural to inquire.

**Daniel 12:7** Updated American Standard Version (UASV)

7 And I heard the man clothed in linen, who was above the waters of the stream; he raised his right hand and his left hand toward heaven and swore by him who lives forever that it would be for a time, times, and half a time,[73] and that when the shattering of the power of the holy people comes to an end all these things would be finished.

**And I heard the man clothed in linen –** Gabriel not only replied at once to the question but in such a way as though it was a grand and far-reaching truth regarding the future.

**he raised his right hand and his left hand toward heaven –** Gabriel reaches out to the heavens, home of God, seeking the reliability and the truth of what he was about to announce. He was about to make the declaration in the most serious manner imaginable.

**and swore by him who lives forever –** Yes, Gabriel, swore by the eternal God, which simply means that he appealed to him, making the solemn or emphatic declaration or statement before the face of God. He was letting Daniel know that God himself was serving as a witness to the truth of what he was about to disclose. All of this suggests that whatever information

[73] That is, *three and a half times*

Gabriel had to share; was going to have the most significant consequence regarding future events.

**that it would be for a time, times, and half a time** – That is, three and a half times. The expression means three times, or periods, and a half. James A. Montgomery is correct when he observed, "Here, v. 7, it is in the terms of 7:27, with the Heb. equivalent of the Aram. there; *i.e.*, three and a half years."[74] So, the three and a half times in here refer to three and a half years of 365 days each. But when did these 1,278 days begin? Somehow, the number is not like other prophecies that usually deal in rounded or even numbers. But if we like at those three and a half years, or 42 months as lunar months, it would be 1,260 days. This prophecy here in Daniel 12:7 is similar to the prophecies at Daniel 7:25 and at Revelation 11:3, 7, 9. All are prophecies that deal with the time of the end. All deal with the persecution of the holy ones who serve God, and yet they carry on their work of **turning many to righteousness**. Both Daniel 7:25 and 12:7 refer to 'time, times, and half a time.' In Revelation, we have a similar period of 42 months or 1,260 days if counted as lunar months, which seems what was the case. (Revelation 11:2-3)

On this, Kendell H. Easley writes, "42 months; 1,260 days (vv. 2, 3) The Book of Daniel identified a coming intense time of trouble under the phrase "time, times, and half a time" (Dan. 7:25; 12:7). Interpreters agree that he meant three and a half years. If 30 days are allowed for a month, this totals 1,260 days or 42 months. The original readers of Revelation understood instantly when they read these numbers that John was referring to the same thing Daniel had in mind, 'a limited time of great suffering.' What did Daniel and John mean by the phrase? Whatever Daniel had meant, John may have used what had become a contemporary figure of speech, cueing readers or listeners that the period under consideration would be limited but characterized by intense tribulation. Jesus himself adopted this idiom in Luke 4:25, in which he noted that the famine of Elijah's day was just such a 'three and a half years' even though the Old Testament never actually stated the length of the famine. Certainly it is possible that these time references will turn out to be precisely literal, but it is also possible that they do not define the exact length of time of the great tribulation any more than the American idiom 'seven year itch' defines the duration of that condition."[75]

---

[74] James A. Montgomery, *A Critical and Exegetical Commentary on the Book of Daniel*, International Critical Commentary (New York: Charles Scribner's Sons, 1927), 475.

[75] Kendell H. Easley, *Revelation*, vol. 12, Holman New Testament Commentary (Nashville, TN: Broadman & Holman Publishers, 1998), 202.

**and that when the shattering of the power of the holy people comes to an end all these things would be finished –** This is referring to the period this persecution that these holy ones had been facing would come to an end and "all these things would be finished."

**Daniel 12:8-9** Updated American Standard Version (UASV)

[8] I heard, but I did not understand. Then I said, "O my lord, what shall be the outcome of these things?" [9] He said, "Go your way, Daniel, for the words are shut up and sealed until the time of the end.

As we learned earlier, Daniel wrote the book that bears his name, but he could not fully understand them. Even so, he must have been concerned about "the shattering of the power of the holy people." Would they actually be totally destroyed by their persecutors, for he asked, "O my lord, what shall be the outcome of these things?" This time period that is called "the last days" and "the time of the end." (2 Tim. 3:1; Dan 12:4, 9), runs from 33 A.D. up to Armageddon. Michael the archangel has been standing on behalf of God's people in heaven. – Isaiah 11:10; Revelation 12:7-9.

**Daniel 12:10** Updated American Standard Version (UASV)

[10] Many shall purify themselves and make themselves white and be refined, but the wicked shall act wickedly. And none of the wicked shall understand, but those who are wise shall understand.

Daniel had hope for the holy ones! Instead of their being destroyed, they would be made "white and refined." In other words, these holy ones would be made pure, and they would have a clean standing before God. (Mal. 3:1-3) Their new insight into the Scriptures would guide them, helping them to maintain a clean standing in the eyes of God. On the other hand, the wicked would reject the Word of God that these holy ones were sharing.

**Daniel 12:11** Updated American Standard Version (UASV)

[11] And from the time that the continual burnt offering is taken away and the abomination that causes desolation is set up there will be one thousand two hundred and ninety days.

Matthew 24:13 reads, "But **the one who endures <u>to the end</u>** will be saved." Matthew 24:14 said, "this gospel of the kingdom will be proclaimed throughout the whole world as a testimony to all nations, **and then <u>the end will come</u>**." Matthew 24:15 begins with the Greek word *hotan* "whenever" followed by *oun* "therefore, which reads in English, "Therefore when," which connects what preceded, "**the end**," and leads into what follows. Let us take a moment to investigate verse 15.

In verses 3-14, Jesus outlined the signs of "the end of the age." Here in Mathew 24:15, Jesus begins with, "**Therefore when** you see the abomination of desolation, which was spoken of through Daniel the prophet, standing in the holy place (let the reader understand)." If we look at the corresponding accounts in Mark and Luke, they offer us additional insights. Mark 13:14 says, "standing where it ought not to be." Luke 21:20 adds Jesus' words, "But when you see Jerusalem surrounded by armies, then know[76] that its desolation has come near." The complete picture is an "abomination" "standing in the holy place," i.e., "where it ought not be," namely, "Jerusalem surrounded by armies."

This is a reference to the Roman army, which assaulted Jerusalem and its temple starting in 66 C.E., under General Cestus Gallus. The temple was the "holy place," and the abomination was the Roman army "standing where it ought not to be." As for the "desolation" came in 70 C.E. when General Titus of the Roman army completely desolated Jerusalem and its temple. Specifically, what was this "abomination"? Moreover, in what sense was it "standing in the holy place"?

Jesus had urged the readers to *understand*. What was it that they were to *understand*? They were to *understand* that "which was spoken of through Daniel the prophet," i.e., Daniel 9:27. Part "b" of verse 27 reads, "And upon the wing of abominations shall come the one causing desolation, even until a complete destruction, one that is decreed, is poured out on the one causing desolation." – Daniel 9:26-27; see also Daniel 11:31; 12:11.

> The *abomination of desolation* is an expression that recurs in Daniel with some variation in wording (Daniel 8:13; 9:27; 11:31; 12:11), where most scholars agree that there is a reference to the desecration perpetrated by Antiochus Epiphanes when he built an altar to Zeus in the temple and offered swine and other unclean animals on it as sacrifices (cf. 1 Macc. 1:41–61).[77]

Jesus' words were an apparent reference to the Roman armies of 66–70 C.E. It may very well be that Daniel's prophecy points to Antiochus Epiphanes "who in 167 [B.C.E., 200-years before Jesus uttered his prophecy] plundered the temple, ordered the sacrificial system to cease, and polluted the altar of the Lord by turning it into a pagan altar, where unclean sacrifices

[76] Or *then recognize*

[77] Leon Morris, *The Gospel According to Matthew*, The Pillar New Testament Commentary (Grand Rapids, MI; Leicester, England: W.B. Eerdmans; Inter-Varsity Press, 1992), 603.

were offered to pagan deities."[78] Jesus used Daniel's prophecy about Antiochus Epiphanes and gave us an *Inspired Sensus Plenior Application*, by having a whole other meaning, a completely different meaning for those words, making them applicable to the Roman armies desolating Jerusalem between 66 and 70 C.E.

On many occasions, a New Testament writer would quote or cite an Old Testament Scripture. Often, the New Testament writer would be using the Old Testament text contextually, according to the setting and intent of the Old Testament writer (observing the grammatical-historical sense). However, at times the New Testament writer would add to or apply the text differently than what was meant by the Old Testament writer (**not** observing the grammatical-historical sense). This is either a new or a progressive revelation of God. He has inspired the New Testament writer to go beyond the intended meaning of the Old Testament writer and carry out what is known as *Inspired Sensus Plenior Application* (ISPA). In this latter case, the New Testament writer uses the Old Testament text to convey another meaning to another circumstance. This does not violate the principle that all Bible verses have just one single meaning. The Old Testament text has one meaning, and the New Testament writer's adaptation of that text is not a second meaning but another meaning.

What events mark the beginning of the great tribulation? Jesus foretold: "Therefore when you see the abomination of desolation,[79] which was spoken of through Daniel the prophet, standing in the holy place (let the reader understand), then let those who are in Judea flee to the mountains." (Matt. 24:15-16) As we just showed above, the fulfillment of Jesus' words "standing in a holy place" occurred in 66 C.E. when the Roman army ("the abomination of desolation") attacked Jerusalem and its temple (the holy place). Now, we have argued that a verse only has one meaning. Daniel was referring to Antiochus, which is one meaning for Daniel. Jesus' words referring to Daniel, but creating an entirely different meaning, the Roman army attacking Jerusalem. So, how do we get Jesus' words to apply to the great tribulation that culminates into Armageddon? The more significant fulfillment of Daniel and Jesus' words are found in the apostle John's comments in the book of

---

[78] Larry Chouinard, *Matthew*, The College Press NIV Commentary (Joplin, MO: College Press, 1997), Mt 24:15.

[79] **Abomination of Desolation**: (Gr. *bdelugma eremoseos*) An expression by Jesus recorded in Mathew 24:15 and Mark 13:14 referring to Daniel 11:31 and 12:11. *Bdelugma* refers to something that is an abomination, unclean, which horrifies clean persons, leaving them disgusted. *Eremoseos* has the sense of an extensive desolating act or destruction, which caused total ruin, leaving no place for shelter.

Revelation, verses that we already used to establish a connection with Daniel and the three and a half years, or 42 months, or 1,260 days.

**Revelation 11:1-2** Updated American Standard Version (UASV)

**11** Then there was given me a measuring rod like a reed, saying, "Rise and **measure the temple of God** and the altar and those who worship there. 2 But the courtyard that is outside the temple, leave it out and do not measure it, because it has been given to the nations, and they will trample the holy city **for forty-two months**.

The look ahead at another "abomination" in the temple or holy place is yet future. Kendell H. Easley writes, "The imagery of Revelation here is similar to two events in Jewish history, one remote and one more recent. First, pagans literally trampled historical Jerusalem from 168–165 B.C. during the days of the wicked Syrian king Antiochus Epiphanes. (See Daniel 8 and the book of 1 Maccabees in the Apocrypha.) They even took over the inner courts of the temple, offering swine sacrifices. Second, Roman legions had trampled and demolished Jerusalem and its temple in a.d. 70 (Luke 21:24). Both instances involved a Jewish war of some three years' duration. The forty-two months (= 1,260 days = time, times, and half a time = 3.5 years) had become a standardized expression for a limited time of intense suffering. (A typical American standard expression is 'forty-hour week' to express 'fully employed' without necessarily meaning an exact length of time.) God will specially protect his people spiritually during this time, but he will allow many of them to be 'trampled on by the nations,' becoming martyrs for his sake during the terrible times before the return of Christ."[80]

Again, Gabriel says, "from the time that the continual burnt offering is taken away and the abomination that causes desolation is set up there will be **one thousand two hundred and ninety days**." He gives Daniel an exact answer to the question. But what is this event? This continual burnt offering? Under the Mosaic Law, "the continual burnt offering" was burned on the altar at the temple in Jerusalem. Many of the commentators believe that the Jewish people, who have never accepted Christ, will be allowed to survive the great tribulation and Armageddon, right into the millennial kingdom, the thousand-year reign of Christ? This just is **not** the case. This will not be an excursion here where I offer evidence, for it deserves its own chapter to do it justice. So, see the next chapter.

---

[80] Kendell H. Easley, *Revelation*, vol. 12, Holman New Testament Commentary (Nashville, TN: Broadman & Holman Publishers, 1998), 189.

So, we are talking about Christians here, and they do not offer burnt offerings in the temple. However, they are referred to as "Israel of God." (Gal. 6:16) And they do provide continual offerings. Paul said: "Through him then let us continually offer up a sacrifice of praise to God, that is, the fruit of lips that confess his name." (Hebrews 13:15) Paul was referencing Hosea 14:2, "Take words with you and return to Jehovah; say to him, 'Take away all error; accept what is good, and we will offer with bulls the praise of our lips." This evangelizing, the great commission, is the continual offering taken away during the great tribulation for 1,290 days.

**Daniel 12:12** Updated American Standard Version (UASV)

12 Happy is the one who is eagerly waiting and who arrives at the one thousand three hundred and thirty-five days.

Many commentators are taking the three time periods 1,260 days, 1,290 days, and 1,335 days, trying to combine them in some way (as though it is one or two time periods, which creates chronological problems. Instead, I believe that they should be run consecutively. The 1,335 days, or three years, eight and a half months began at the end of the previous 1,290 days, which had followed the previous 1,260 days. This means that the great tribulation will run 3,885 days, 127.7 months, 10.64 years.

*What happened during those 1,335 days?*

**Daniel 12:7 (1,260 days)**: a time of persecution during the great tribulation for the holy ones and yet they turn many to righteousness.

**Daniel 12:11 (1,290 days)**: evangelizing, the great commission is the continual offering that will be taken away for some time during the great tribulation.

**Daniel 12:12 (1,335 days)**: the holy ones find happiness as the great tribulation closes, knowing Jesus' words, "the one who endures to the end will be saved." (Matthew 24:13) Jesus' words fit well with the angel's closing words to Daniel in 12:13.

The holy ones of Daniel chapter 12 are genuine Christians in general. Still, Satan's world powers, the King of the North, will be primarily focused on the "chosen ones" that Jesus spoke of, which are those who have been chosen out of true Christians by God to rule as kings, priests, and judges with Christ for a literal thousand years.

**Daniel 12:13** Updated American Standard Version (UASV)

13 But go your way till the end; and you shall rest and shall stand in your allotted place at the end of the days."

These words seem to suggest that Daniel's life was coming to a close, and the angel was assuring him of a resurrection.

Daniel had served God far more faithfully than most other Old Testament persons who were considered righteous. Daniel was faithful **till the end** of his life. Now he is asleep in death, but he will **stand up** in "the resurrection of the righteous ones" during the thousand-year reign of Christ Jesus. – Luke 14:14; Acts 24:15.

# CHAPTER 6 Are the Natural Jews Today Still God's Chosen People?

When James speaks of "the twelve tribes in the Dispersion," he is not referring to the 12 tribes of literal Israel, as the Jews, who made up Judaism were not his "brothers" that were 'holding the faith in our Lord Jesus Christ.' (See James 1:2; 2:1, 5) Before Jesus' execution, He made it clear that the 12 tribes of literal Israel had been rejected. He said, "the kingdom of God will be taken away from you and given to a people producing its fruits." (Matt. 21:43) Who are these people that would produce fruit? It was "the Israel of God." (Gal 6:16) After Jesus' ransom sacrifice, those who entered the Christian congregation were not Jews in a fleshly way but were the Israel of God in an inward way, a spiritual Israel, open to both Jew and Gentile. (Rom. 2:29; 4:16, 17; 9:6-8; Gal. 3:7, 29; 4:21-31; Phil. 3:3) These spiritual Israelites were dispersed throughout the then known world. "There arose on that day a great persecution against the church in Jerusalem, and they were all scattered throughout the regions of Judea and Samaria, except the apostles." (Ac 8:1) So after that, through these scattered ones and the work of the evangelists, congregations were being started all through the Roman Empire. In fact, we find Peter using the same words as James, "the Dispersion in Pontus, Galatia, Cappadocia, Asia, and Bithynia." (1 Pet. 1:1) Therefore, Jews were living in dispersed nations at the time of James' writing. Whatever the case, James' letter is writing to Christians going through trials of many various kinds.

The sons of Israel in the first-century responded positively to the preaching of Jesus and his apostles. (Acts 10:36) The same holds true for today. However, we have **Messianic Judaism**, a movement that combines Christianity, most importantly, the Christian belief that Jesus is the Messiah, with elements of **Judaism** and **Jewish** tradition. This is not going to be acceptable, though, as Jesus told them, we are not trying to put new wine in an old wineskin. First, we must deal with the fact of whether the Jews are still God's chosen people.

## Are the Natural Jews Today Still God's Chosen People?

**To the twelve tribes in the Dispersion: (James 1:1c)**

The **twelve tribes in the dispersion** that James mentions are not actually the 12 tribes of Israel. We note in verse 2 James says, "Consider it all joy, my brothers," and the tribes of Jewish Israel were not James' brother, 'who were holding their faith in their glorious Lord Jesus Christ, as natural Israel rejected Jesus Christ vehemently. (Jam. 1:2; 2:1, 5) During the last days of Jesus' ministry, he explicitly stated what would happen to natural Israel. Jesus said, "I tell you, the kingdom of God will be taken away from you and given to a people producing its fruits." (Matt. 21:43) A short time later, he said,

**Matthew 23:37-39** Updated American Standard Version (UASV)

**Lament over Jerusalem**

37 "Jerusalem, Jerusalem, who kills the prophets and stones those who are sent to her! How often I wanted to gather your children together, the way a hen gathers her chicks under her wings, and you were unwilling.

38 Behold, your house is being left to you desolate!

39 For I say to you, from now on you will not see me until you say, 'Blessed is he who comes in the name of the Lord.'"

In looking at verse 37 of Matthew 23, we see that Jesus' words are not those of a harsh judge, who is looking ready to punish the Jewish people for their 1,500 years of rebelling and sinning horrendously against the Father. Instead, he has tried to be patient with them throughout his last three and half year ministry. When Jesus began his ministry, all Jesus wanted was nothing more than what his Father wanted, i.e., repentance for centuries of willful sinning, so that they could avoid the judgment that was coming. Well, over five hundred natural Israel responded to Jesus' words, with thousands upon thousands more listening to the apostle Paul and other evangelists. They escaped the judgment that came upon Jerusalem in 70 C.E. (Lu 21:20-22) In verse 38, Jesus indicated that very soon God was not going to accept the worship of the Israelites at the typical temple in Jerusalem. (Matt 24:1-2) In verse 39, Jesus is saying they will never see him with eyes of faith unless they accept him and his Father.

In other words, natural Israel lost its favored position as God's chosen people, and this was to be given to another. Who? This new nation proved to be a spiritual Israel, which the apostle Paul referred to as "the Israel of God." It would be made up of Jews who accepted Jesus Christ and non-Jews. Entry into this "Israel of God" was not dependent on a natural descent, but rather on one coming to "know you the only true God, and Jesus Christ whom you have sent." (John 17:3), In other words, it was a matter of 'trusting in Jesus Christ.' (John 3:16) Nevertheless, natural Israel was made up of 12 tribes, so James was simply drawing on the number 12, which carries the connotation of completeness. If a natural Jew or a non-Jew were to become a part of this spiritual Israel, the Israel of God, they would have to acknowledge, "Circumcision is a matter of the heart, by the Spirit, not by the letter." (Rom. 2:29) He must further understand "it depends on faith, in order that the promise may rest on grace and be guaranteed to all …" (Rom. 4:16) There are many verses, which qualify what it means to be a part of this Israel of God. See also, Rom. 4:17; 9:6-8; Gal. 3:7, 29; 4:21-31; Phil. 3:3

These spiritual Israelites were dispersed throughout the Roman Empire. Shortly after Pentecost 33 C.E., there were arrests, threats, and beatings. (Ac 4:1-3, 21; 5:17, 18) At that time, Stephen was seized and stoned to death. " (Ac 7:52-60) The murder of Stephen was only the beginning, as Saul of Tarsus was to bring great persecution of the Christians in the Jerusalem area, which led to the dispersing of Christians throughout the then known world. (Ac 8:1-4; 9:1, 2) However, this really failed, as it was not long before Christian congregations were found everywhere. The evangelism of none other than the very persecutor turned Christian, namely, the apostle Paul (formerly known as Saul). In fact, about 62-64 C.E., Peter writes, "To those who are elect exiles of the Dispersion in Pontus, Galatia, Cappadocia, Asia, and Bithynia." – 1 Peter 1:1

## Written for Our Instruction

We can learn some object lessons from what God has disclosed to us in his Word. Paul told the Corinthians, "these things happened to those people as an example but are written for our instruction." (1 Cor. 10:11) He also told the congregation in Rome, "For whatever was written beforehand was written for our instruction, so that through patient endurance and through the encouragement of the scriptures we may have hope." (Rom. 15:4) The Israelites are a perfect example for us to learn. God chose Abraham, Isaac, and Jacob personally because they were walking with him, while others chose to abandon him. The nation of Israel was the descendants of Jacob's 12 sons. They became God's chosen people, of whom he made a covenant, to which they agreed to follow. If they walked in the truth, they would be blessed by Jehovah's presence. If they abandoned that walk like the pagan nations, they would lose his presence, resulting in the difficulties of living in this fallen world. While they maintained their loyalty, they never became victims to enemy nations. (Deut. 28:7) Furthermore, they could depend on crop growth that was exceptional year after year, as well as their flocks of animals. (Ex. 22:1-15) Moreover, they had no reason to build jails to house criminals because they had the perfect social system. (Ex. 22:1-15) In addition, they did not suffer from diseases like other nations (Deut. 7:15). Jehovah promised them that they would "be blessed more than all of the peoples," and when they walked in the truth, this proved to be true.

**Deuteronomy 7:14** Updated American Standard Version (UASV)

14 You shall be blessed above all peoples; there will be no male or female barren among you or among your cattle.

We all have the history before of how Israel **refused** to walk in the truth. They would walk in the truth for a number of years, and then they would abandon that truth until life was impossibly difficult, moving them to return to Jehovah. This walking in the truth, abandoning the truth, and repenting to return to the truth, went on for 1,500 years. The final difficulty in this back and forth was their rejection of the Son of God. His words to them were quite clear and needs to be repeated again:

**Matthew 21:43** Updated American Standard Version (UASV)

43 Therefore I say to you, the kingdom of God will be taken away from you and **given to a nation,**[81] **producing the fruit** of it.

Again,

**Matthew 23:37-39** Updated American Standard Version (UASV)

37 "Jerusalem, Jerusalem, who kills the prophets and stones those who are sent to her! How often I wanted to gather your children together, the way a hen gathers her chicks under her wings, and you were unwilling.

38 Behold, your house is being left to you desolate!

39 For I say to you, from now on you will not see me until you say, 'Blessed is he who comes in the name of the Lord.'"

Just who are **the people** that the Kingdom was to be given to after the Israelites fell out of favor with Jehovah God? God chose for himself a new spiritual nation, which became the Christian congregation that Jesus established between 29 and 33 C.E. He no longer had the descendants of Abraham, Isaac, and Jacob as his chosen people, by which other nations would bless themselves. Keep in mind again, only Jews were brought into the Christian congregation from 29 C.E. (Jesus started ministry) up unto 36 C.E. (first Gentile Baptized, i.e., Cornelius). This is explained in greater detail below.

---

[81] Or *people*

**Acts 10:34-35** Updated American Standard Version (UASV)

34 So Peter opened his mouth and said: "Truly I understand that God shows no partiality, 35 but in every nation anyone who fears[82] him and works righteousness[83] is acceptable to him.

**Acts 13:46** Updated American Standard Version (UASV)

46 And Paul and Barnabas spoke out boldly and said, "It was necessary that the word of God be spoken to you first; since you thrust it aside and judge yourselves unworthy of eternal life, behold, we are turning to the Gentiles.

Did this mean that no Jewish person could be a part of the Kingdom? Hardly! For seven years, 29 C.E. to 36 C.E., the first disciples of that Kingdom were only Jewish people. After 36 C.E. and the baptism of the first Gentile, Cornelius, anyone, including the Jews, could be a part of this Kingdom as long as they accepted the King, Jesus Christ. Jesus said, "I am the way, and the truth, and the life. No one comes to the Father except through me." (John 14:6) At Jesus' Baptism, there was a voice from heaven saying, "This is my beloved Son, with whom I am well pleased." (Matt.3:16-17) Jesus' teaching, miraculous signs, his ransom sacrifice, and resurrection established him as the truth, having the authority and power of the Father.[84] The Christians in the first century were given the position of being God's chosen people. (Acts 1:8; 2:1-4, 43) It would be through Jesus to the Christian congregation that the truth would now flow. As Paul told the Corinthians, "For to us God has revealed them through the Spirit. For the Spirit searches all things, even the depths of God." (1 Cor. 2:10) It happened just as Jesus had said it would, "I praise you, Father, Lord of heaven and earth because you have hidden these things from the wise and intelligent, and have revealed them to young children." – Matthew 11:25

However, more truth was on the horizon with the birth of the Christian congregation. There had been 39 books written by the Jewish writers of the Hebrew Old Testament (2 Tim. 3:16-17), and now there was to be added an additional 27 books by Jewish Christians, making up the Greek New Testament (2 Peter 2:15-16). Thus, 66 small books, written over a 1,600-year period, would make one book, which we hold today in our modern-day translations. Yes, some 40 plus Bible writers were, as Peter put it, "men carried along by the Holy Spirit spoke from God." (2 Peter 1:21) The above

[82] This is a reverential fear of displeasing God because of one's great love for him. It is not a dreadful fear.

[83] That is, *does what is right*

[84] Matt. 15:30-31; 20:28; John 4:34; 5:19, 27, 30; 6:38, 40; 7:16-17; 17:1-2; Acts 2:22

view is Scriptural, but it is also the minority view. Most believe as Dr. Elmer Towns,

> Israel's hardness of heart. The Bible speaks of a partial and temporary insensibility of the nation of Israel. The Jews, who had the Scriptures and should have welcomed their Messiah, rejected him and called for his crucifixion. "He (Jesus) came unto his own (the Jews), and his own received him not" (John 1:11). Paul spoke of "blindness (hardness)" as happening to Israel (Rom. 11:25). Israel's rejection is temporary. The time is coming when many Jews will turn to Christ (Rom. 11:26; 2 Cor. 3:14, 15). God's temporarily setting aside the nation he loves so much ought to be a warning to Christians not to reject the teaching of the Scriptures.[85]

Elmer Towns says, "Israel's rejection is temporary. The time is coming when many Jews will turn to Christ." They had 1,500 years as God's chosen people, favored in every way, and they abandoned God at every turn, to the point of sacrificing their own children to false gods, culminating in the rejection of the Son of God. He said he had come specifically for them. Moreover, John himself says that anyone or group who rejects Jesus Christ is the Antichrist (i.e., instead of or against Christ). The Messianic Jews do accept Christ, so most would think they are fine. However, that just is not the case because it is **combining it** with elements of **Judaism** and **Jewish** tradition. What did Jesus say about Jewish tradition? He said you are "making void the word of God by your tradition that you have handed down." (Mark 13:7) Let us look at Jesus' words at Luke 5:38, "But new wine must be put into fresh wineskins." What did Jesus mean?

> The conclusion of the second picture is stated positively: new wine must have new skins; new ways must have new containers. Jesus' teaching will not survive by making it conform to old ways. A new form, a new spirit, and a new approach are required. Old questions are irrelevant. Such a message had relevance beyond the time of Jesus' ministry. In the early church and throughout the new age, to re-Judaize Christianity would have missed the newness of what Jesus brings. The issue raised here is one of the major concerns in the Book of Acts, as the church wrestles with the proper limits of the influence of its Jewish heritage. The focus is not on a return to something old and ancient, but on the presence of something new. This does not mean that some forms of the old worship, like fasting, cannot continue; but it does mean that they

[85] Towns, Elmer (2011-10-30). AMG Concise Bible Doctrines (AMG Concise Series) (Kindle Locations 960-965). AMG Publishers. Kindle Edition.

are seen differently. The remarks fit the situation in Jesus' ministry, but the significance became timeless for the church's perspective.[86] (Bock 1994, p. 521)

The actual way to God was through the Israelite nation for over 1,500 years. When Jesus arrived, he began what would become known as Christianity, his followers being called Christian.

**Matthew 9:16-17** Updated American Standard Version (UASV)

16 But no one puts a patch of unshrunk cloth on an old garment; for the patch pulls away from the garment, and the tear becomes worse. 17 Nor do they put new wine into old wineskins. If they do, then the wineskins burst and the wine spills out and the wineskins are ruined. But they do put new wine into new wineskins, and both are preserved."

Jesus was making a point to the disciples of John the Baptist that no one should expect the followers of Jesus Christ to try to retain the old practices of Judaism, such as ritualistic fasting. A Christian can fast if he chooses to do so, but there are no obligations to do so. Jesus did not come to patch up the old ways of worship by way of Judaism, which would be set aside on the day of Jesus' ransom sacrifice. Christianity is not to conform to the old way of worship, to the form Jewish religious system, with the traditions of men.

As Jesus said, Christianity was not going to be a new patch on an old garment or a new wine in an old wineskin. Any Christian or so-called Jewish Christian, who tries to suggest mixing the two, is nothing more than false prophets. – Matthew 24:11.

The greatest misidentification has been the interpretation that the Antichrist and the man of lawlessness are just one particular person. We can define antichrist as anyone, any group, any organization, or any government that is against or instead of Christ or who mistreat his people. Thus, we are not just looking for one person, group, organization, or power. The Bible does not refer to just one antichrist.

After the destruction of Jerusalem in 70 C.E., up unto this day, the Jews *have not put faith* in Jesus Christ, the Son of God, but have rather continued their search for a Messiah in the flesh. This is not to say that no individual Jewish persons have not converted to Christianity, as hundreds of thousands have in the last two millennia.

---

[86] Paul raises such issues in 1 Cor. 7:17–24; 8–11; and Rom. 14–15. While not rejecting Jewish worship forms, he did not regard them as required. His approach parallels Jesus'.

**Will the Jews in the last days, or during the great tribulation, finally be moved to accept Jesus Christ?**

**Romans 11:25-26** Good News Translation (GNT)

25 There is a secret truth, my friends, which I want you to know, for it will keep you from thinking how wise you are. It is that the stubbornness of the people of Israel is not permanent, but will last only until the complete number of Gentiles comes to God.
26 And **this is how** all Israel will be saved. As the scripture says,

"The Savior will come from Zion
and remove all wickedness from the descendants of Jacob."

Notice the GNT says, "this is how (ESV, HCSB, "and in this way") Greek, *houtos*] all Israel will be saved." In addition, notice that this "**all Israel** will be saved" is not accomplished by some conversion of all the Jews, but rather "the complete number of Gentiles comes to God." A Manual Greek Lexicon of the New Testament [Edinburgh, 1937, G. Abbott-Smith, p. 329] defines *houtos* as meaning "in this way, so, thus."). In addition, *A TRANSLATOR'S HANDBOOK ON PAUL'S LETTER TO THE ROMANS* [New York, 1973, United Bible Societies, p. 227], says, "*This is how* relates back to what Paul has previously said."

If we are to understand Romans 11:25-26 correctly, it must be in the context of the book of Romans as a whole and the rest of the New Testament. What did Paul say at Romans 2:28-28, "For no one is a Jew who is merely one outwardly, nor is circumcision outward and physical. But a Jew is one inwardly, and circumcision is a matter of the heart, by the Spirit, not by the letter. His praise is not from man but from God." In Romans 9:26, Paul says, "For not all those who are descended from Israel are truly Israel."

What about the Abrahamic covenant argument assures that the Jews will always be God's chosen people.

**Galatians 3:27-29** New American Standard Bible (NASB)

27 For all of you who were baptized into Christ have clothed yourselves with Christ.
28 There is neither Jew nor Greek, there is neither slave nor free man, there is neither male nor female; for you are all one in Christ Jesus.
29 And *if you belong to Christ, then you are Abraham's descendants*, heirs according to promise. (Italics mine)

Here we see things from God's perspective. It is not a matter of being a natural descendant of Abraham that makes one a part of Abraham's seed.

**Are the things going on in Israel today and until Christ's return a part of Bible prophecy?**

**Ezekiel 37:21-22** Updated American Standard Version (UASV)

[21] then say to them, Thus says the Lord Jehovah: Behold, I will take the sons of Israel from the nations among which they have gone, and I will gather them from every side and bring them into their own land [22] and I will make them one nation in the land, on the mountains of Israel; and one king will be king for all of them; and they will no longer be two nations and no longer be divided into two kingdoms.

Israel has not been under one king of the line of David for well over 2,300 years. The state of Israel today is a republic.

**Isaiah 2:2-4** Updated American Standard Version (UASV)

[2] It will come to pass in the latter days
that the mountain of the house of Jehovah
will be established on the top of the mountains,
and will be lifted up above the hills;
and all the nations will stream to it,
3 and many peoples will come, and say:
"Come, let us go up to the mountain of Jehovah,
to **the house of the God of Jacob**,
that he may teach us concerning his ways
and that we may walk in his paths."
For the law[87] will go forth from Zion,
and the word of Jehovah from Jerusalem.
[4] He will judge between the nations,
and will correct matters for many peoples;
and they shall beat their swords into plowshares,
and their spears into pruning hooks;
nation shall not lift up sword against nation,
neither shall they learn war anymore.

What do we find when we look at the city of Jerusalem today? Do we find "the house of the God of Jacob"? No, we do not; rather we find an Islamic shrine. Certainly, living in the heart of Islamic nations, they would not ever dream of "beat[ing] their swords into plowshares."

[87] Or *instruction* or *teaching*

**Zechariah 8:23** Updated American Standard Version (USV)

23 This is what Jehovah of armies says: In those days ten men from the nations of every tongue[88] shall take hold of the garment of a man who is a Jew, saying, 'Let us go with you, for we have heard that God is with you.'"

**Zechariah 8:23** American Standard Version (ASV)

23 Thus says **Jehovah** of hosts: In those days it shall come to pass, that ten men shall take hold, out of all the languages of the nations, they shall take hold of the skirt of him that is a Jew, saying, We will go with you, for we have heard that God is with you.

**Zechariah 8:23** Young's Literal Translation (YLT)

23 Thus said **Jehovah** of Hosts: In those days take hold do ten men of all languages of the nations, Yea, they have taken hold on the skirt of a man, a Jew, saying: We go with you, for we heard God [is] with you!

Within the book of Zechariah alone, the personal name of God (Jehovah JHVH, or Yahweh YHWH) appears 130 times. If you are ever around an orthodox Jew, say Jehovah or Yahweh, and he will jump back and say something like, "we do not say the blessed name." Jews, because of traditions and superstitions have not said the personal name of God for about 2,000 years. It is to the point that it has even been removed from almost all English translations, replacing it with the title "the Lord" or "LORD." These prophecies of a restored Israel, who do they apply to, natural Israel?

**Galatians 6:15-16** Updated American Standard Version (UASV)

15 For neither circumcision counts for anything, nor uncircumcision, but a new creation.16 And as for all who walk by this rule, peace and mercy be upon them, and upon **the Israel of God**.

This "Israel of God" is not based on the requirements that Abraham had received from God, i.e., all males having to be circumcised. Instead, as was stated in 3:26-29, "there are neither Jew nor Greek, … for you are all one in Christ Jesus. **29** And *if you belong to Christ, then you are Abraham's descendants*, heirs according to promise."

### The Average Jewish Person

It should be noted that the average Jew we might run into is generally a faithful follower of the traditions of Rabbis, and doctrinal views are likely not of interest. Somewhat like how the Catholic Church views the word of the

---

[88] hat is, *the languages*

pope to be equal to Scripture, this would be true of the average Jew and Rabbi traditions. Therefore, while we might have thought we could have had some deep Bible discussion to build rapport, this is unlikely. In addition, the word "Bible" is generally viewed as a Christian book. It is for this reason; it is best to talk about the Hebrew Scriptures, even the "Torah." If anyone can read biblical Hebrew, which I know there are a limited number, his or her success of reading from the Hebrew Scriptures directly would be very successful with the Orthodox Jews, who will seldom give a Christian the time of day.

Well, we might be wondering just what can we talk about with the average Jewish person. They hold that there is one God, monotheism, who is interested in the welfare of his creation. However, it is best not to use the personal name of God ("Jehovah" or "Yahweh"), as one of their traditions is that the divine name should not be pronounced. They, like Christians, believe that God has involved himself in human history and continued to do so. Some Jewish people struggle with why God would allow the atrocities of six million Jews being slaughtered during the Holocaust of World War II.[89] Most are aware of the history of the Hebrew Scriptures, which makes for many talking points.

Of course, it is best to stay away from Jesus being divine, but many Jews do see Jesus as a prophet. It might be best not to refer to him as the Messiah, even though that is the Hebrew transliteration and preferable to "Christ." The reason is the Jewish people are still awaiting the Messiah. This deep discussion would have to wait until we have talked with someone many times and have built up much rapport and trust. To begin with, it would be better, such ones as Noah, Abraham, and Moses, and their role in Jewish history and how it affects us today.

When the time comes to address Jesus as the Messiah, we would want, to begin with, Deuteronomy 18:15 (UASV), which reads, "Jehovah your God will raise up for you a prophet like me from among you, from your brothers to him you shall listen." Then, ask the person, "Who was it that Moses was thinking of when he spoke of a prophet like himself?" "How should this prophecy be understood?" [Allow for an answer] Ask/state, "You would agree that Moses was speaking of a specific, special individual, right?" [Allow for an answer] I know some Jewish scholars have held that Moses was just making a general comment about God's intention to rise up many coming prophets, but the Hebrew word for prophet (navi) is in the singular is it not?" [Allow for an answer] "This coming one is being compared to Moses in what

[89] IF GOD IS GOOD: Why Does God Allow Suffering? – March 24, 2015 by Edward D Andrews (**ISBN-13** : 978-0692414620)

way?" [Allow for an answer] Then, have him read the closing words of Deuteronomy,

**Deuteronomy 34:10-12** Updated American Standard Version (UASV)

[10] Since that time no prophet has risen in Israel like Moses, whom Jehovah knew face to face, [11] for all the signs and wonders which Jehovah sent him to perform in the land of Egypt against Pharaoh, all his servants, and all his land, [12] and for the mighty hand[90] and for all the great wonders which Moses performed in the sight of all Israel.

Ask him if he would agree that it was like Joshua, the son of Nun, who recorded these words about Moses. [Allow for an answer] Ask, if he feels that Joshua, who was a great leader in Israel, viewed himself as the coming prophet like Moses. [Allow for an answer] Ask again, "what do you think Moses meant that God would raise up a prophet like Moses?" "In other words, what was it about Moses that this coming one would resemble?" [Allow for an answer]

We could then delve into how Moses was a great leader; he was a representative of God, "a prophet, a miracle worker, a teacher, and a judge."[91] We could ask a series of leading questions. What did Jeremiah promise at 31:31-34?

**Jeremiah 31:31-34** Updated American Standard Version (UASV)

[31] "Behold, days are coming," declares Jehovah, "when I will make a new covenant with the house of Israel and with the house of Judah, [32] not like the covenant which I made with their fathers in the day I took them by the hand to bring them out of the land of Egypt, My covenant which they broke, although I was a husband to them," declares Jehovah. [33] For this is the covenant that I will make with the house of Israel after those days, declares Jehovah: I will put my law within them, and I will write it on their hearts. And I will be their God, and they shall be my people. [34] And no longer shall each one teach his neighbor and each his brother, saying, 'Know Jehovah,' for they shall all know me, from the least of them to the greatest, declares Jehovah. For I will forgive their iniquity, and I will remember their sin no more."

"What was this new covenant, and what was its purpose?" [Allow for an answer] "When was the new covenant to come into effect?" [Allow for an answer] "Consequently, what would happen to the Mosaic Law?"

---

[90] That is, *mighty power*

[91] Crucifixion or Cruci-Fiction ? (genesis, quotes, baptize .., http://www.city-data.com/forum/religion-spirituality/507377-crucifixion-cruci-fi (accessed September 16, 2015).

What is promised in Jeremiah 31:31-34? What was the new covenant's stated purpose? Consequently, what would become of the Law covenant? [Allow for an answer] How was this new covenant going to affect the nations?" (Read Gen. 22:18) [Allow for an answer] This type of building and leading will evidence your familiarity with the Hebrew Scripture and give him something to ponder.

## Supersessionism / Replacement Theology

Supersessionism, also called replacement theology, is a Christian doctrine that asserts that the New Covenant through Jesus Christ supersedes the Old Covenant, which was made exclusively with the Jewish people.

Theologian Millard J. Erickson explains,

> In Romans 9 and Galatians 3, for example, it is difficult to escape the conclusion that Paul regarded the church, Jew and Gentile alike, as the true heir to the promises originally made to national Israel. It does appear that there will be a period of special favor toward the Jews and that they will in large numbers turn to God. It seems likely, however, that this will be brought about through their being converted and integrated into the church rather than through God resuming the relationship He had with them, as the chosen or covenant nation, in the Old Testament.[92]

Kaiser paints the following developmental picture in the early church: "Replacement theology is not a new arrival in the theological arena, for it probably has its origins in an early political-ecclesiastical alliance forged between Eusebius Pamphilius and the Emperor Constantine. Constantine, regarding himself as God's representative in his role as emperor, gathered all the bishops together on the day of his tricennalia (30th anniversary of his reign), an event, incidentally, which he saw as the foreshadowing of the eschatological Messianic banquet. The results of that meeting, in Eusebius' mind, made it unnecessary to distinguish any longer between the Church and the Empire, for they appeared to merge into one fulfilled kingdom of God on earth in the present time. Such a maneuver, of course, nicely evacuated the role and the significance of the Jewish people in any kingdom considerations. Here began the long trail of replacement theology."[93]

---

[92] Millard J. Erickson, *A Basic Guide to Eschatology* (Grand Rapids: Baker, 1998) 123–24.

[93] Walter C. Kaiser, Jr., "An Assessment of 'Replacement Theology,'" Mishkan (No. 21; 1994), p. 9.

Walter Kaiser tells us that replacement theology "declared that the Church, Abraham's spiritual seed, had replaced national Israel in that it had transcended and fulfilled the terms of the covenant given to Israel, which covenant Israel had lost because of disobedience."[94]

Those **who do not support** the biblically sound Replacement Theology are largely suggesting that those **who do support** it are condemning the Jewish people to some kind of condemnatory judgment where they have no hope. This simply isn't the case. All hope in eternal life lies in our giving ourselves over to Jesus Christ as the Divine Son of God. This applies to every human being. They must accept the Divine Son of God as their personal Savior. This applies to the atheist, the Agnostic, the Muslim, the Hindu, and so on. It also applies to the Jewish people. They have to accept Jesus Christ. We do not allow Muslims to walk in between the Islamic Faith and Christianity. We do not say to Muslims that they can cling to the Quran and Allah as long as they accept Jesus Christ, whom they believe to be only a prophet, and this is acceptable faith in Christ. Therefore, we do not say to the Jewish people that they can cling to Judaism and the Talmud, as long as they accept Jesus Christ, whom they believe to be only a human Jewish teacher, not the long-awaited Messiah this is acceptable faith in Christ. The Jewish people must fully accept Christ as their Lord and Savior and Christianity as the new way to God the Father and abandon the old wine that cannot be put in the new wineskin. When Jesus said this, he was making a point to the disciples of John the Baptist that no one should expect the followers of Jesus Christ to try to retain the old practices of Judaism, such as ritualistic fasting.

---

[94] Walter C. Kaiser, Jr., "An Assessment of 'Replacement Theology,'" Mishkan (No. 21; 1994), p. 9.

# APPENDIX A What Does the Bible Really Say About the Rapture?

The word "**rapture**" occurs nowhere in the Bible. But those who believe in the resurrection of believers to heaven at the Second Coming of Christ cite the apostle Paul's words at 1 Thessalonians 4:17 to support their belief. The Bible shows that before the start of the millennium (thousand-year reign of Christ), there will be a period called the "great tribulation." Jesus said, "For then there will be great tribulation, such as has not been from the beginning of the world until now, no, and never will be." (Matthew 24:21; Revelation 20:6) The rapture ahead of the great tribulation.

**The Rapture** takes place just before the millennium (thousand-year reign of Christ), where Christ will begin the resurrection of those asleep in death. Christ's resurrection of these holy ones from death will occur at the start of the great tribulation and continue as other holy ones died throughout up until just before the start of Armageddon. Some within the church in Thessalonica had died. So, we find the apostle Paul comforting and encouraging the living members with the *resurrection hope.* He wrote, "But we do not want you to be ignorant,[95] brothers, about those who are sleeping in death,[96] so that you will not grieve as do the rest who have no hope." (**1 Thess. 4:13**) He then reminds them, "Jesus died and rose again, even so God will bring with him those fallen asleep in death through[97] Jesus." (**1 Thess. 4:14**) Paul then informs them, "For this we say to you by the word of the Lord, that we who are alive, who remain until the coming of the Lord, will not precede those who have fallen asleep." (**1 Thess. 4:15**) In other words, at the start of the great tribulation, Christ will resurrect those who have been asleep in death first. He explains this in **1 Thess. 4:16**, "For the Lord himself will descend from heaven with a cry of command, with the voice of an archangel, and with the sound of the trumpet of God, and the dead in Christ will rise first." Thus, those faithful Christians among the Thessalonians and

---

[95] Or *uninformed*

[96] Lit (κοιμωμένων koimōmenōn) ones sleeping, i.e., falls asleep in death

[97] **Presence; Coming**: (παρουσία parousia) The Greek word which is rendered as "presence" is derived from *para*, meaning "with," and *ousia*, meaning "being." It denotes both an "arrival" and a consequent "presence with." Depending on the context, it can mean "presence," "arrival," "appearance," or "coming." In some contexts, this word is describing the presence of Jesus Christ in the last days, i.e., from his ascension in 33 C.E. up unto his second coming, with the emphasis being on his second coming, the end of the age of Satan's reign of terror over the earth. We do not know the day nor the hours of this second coming. (Matt 24:36) It covers a marked period of time with the focus on the end of that period. – Matt. 24:3, 27, 37, 39; 1 Cor. 15:23; 16:17; 2 Cor. 7:6-7; 10:10; Php 1:26; 2:12; 1 Thess. 2:19; 3:13; 4:15; 5:2.

all up unto just before the great tribulation who have died would be resurrected first to be with Christ. Following this, just before Armageddon, "Then we who are alive, who remain will be caught up together with them in the clouds to meet the Lord in the air, and so we shall always be with the Lord." (**1 Thess. 4:17**) Who are the ones "who are alive"? Those "who are alive" would be those alive during the great tribulation. They are to be "caught away" "to meet the Lord."

"Caught away," how? Who are these ones "caught up together with them in the clouds to meet the Lord"? These are the holy ones with a heavenly hope who are alive just before Armageddon. If we look at Romans 6:3-5 and 1 Corinthians 15:35, 36, 44, these holy ones must die before they can be resurrected to heaven. However, unlike the Thessalonians and many other Christians who had been asleep in death for 2,000 years or less, these holy ones do not need to remain dead awaiting the second coming of Christ. Paul says of such ones, "Look, I tell you a mystery; we will not all sleep in death,[98] but we will all be changed, [52] in a moment, in the twinkling of an eye …" – 1 Cor. 15:51-52; See Revelation 14:13.

Therefore, the term "rapture" should not be used here because it sends the wrong message as to what the Bible says. Yes, those who are alive at the time who will be serving with Christ as kings, priests, and judges, ruling **over** the earth for a thousand years (Rev. 5:9-10), will be caught up together with them in the clouds to meet the Lord in the air. – 1 Thessalonians 4:7.

Evangelical Dictionary of Theology says,

> **New Heavens and New Earth.** The biblical doctrine of the created universe includes the certainty of its final redemption from the domination of sin. The finally redeemed universe is called "the new heavens and new earth."
>
> In the OT the kingdom of God is usually described in terms of a redeemed earth; this is especially clear in the book of Isaiah, where the final state of the universe is already called new heavens and a new earth (65:17; 66:22). The nature of this renewal was perceived only very dimly by the OT authors, but they did express the belief that a human's ultimate destiny is an earthly one. This vision is clarified in the NT. Jesus speaks of the "renewal" of the world (Matt. 19:28), Peter of the restoration of all things (Acts 3:21). Paul writes that the universe will be redeemed by God from its current state of bondage (Rom. 8:18–21). This is confirmed by

---

[98] lit (*koimēthēsometha*) sleep, i.e., sleep in death

> Peter, who describes the new heavens and the new earth as characterized by righteousness and as the Christian's hope (2 Pet. 3:13). Finally, the book of Revelation includes a glorious vision of the end of the present universe and of the creation of a new universe, full of righteousness and of the presence of God. The vision is confirmed by God in the awesome declaration: "I am making everything new!" (Rev. 21:1–8).
>
> The new heavens and the new earth will be the renewed creation that will fulfill the purpose for which God created the universe. It will be characterized by the complete rule of God and by the full realization of the final goal of redemption: "Now the dwelling of God is with men" (Rev. 21:3).
>
> The fact that the universe will be created anew shows that God's goal for humans is not an ethereal and disembodied existence, but a bodily existence on a perfected earth. The scene of the beatific vision is the new earth. The spiritual does not exclude the created order and will be fully realized only within a perfected creation.[99]

God created the earth to be inhabited, to be filled with perfect humans, who are over the animals, and under the sovereignty of God. (Gen 1:28; 2:8, 15; Ps 104:5; 115:16; Eccl 1:4) Sin did not dissuade God from his plans (Isa. 45:18); hence, he has saved redeemable humankind by Jesus' ransom sacrifice. It seems that the Bible offers two hopes to humans who have been redeemed, **(1) a heavenly hope** or **(2) an earthly hope**. It also seems that those with the heavenly hope are limited in number and are going to heaven to rule with Christ as kings, priests, and judges either **on** the earth or **over** the earth from heaven. The latter, over the earth, fits better with the context and the Greek. It seems that those with the earthly hope are going to receive eternal life here on a paradise earth as it was originally intended.

For almost all faithful Christians, what is the true resurrection hope? It is not a rapture. Instead, they have an earthly hope of eternal life on earth under Jesus Christ as king of God's Kingdom.

---

[99] Walter A. Elwell, *Evangelical Dictionary of Theology: Second Edition* (Grand Rapids, MI: Baker Academic, 2001), 828–829.

# APPENDIX B What Does the Bible Really Say About the Millennium?

The millennium is the kingdom of Christ Jesus and his elect or chosen ones (i.e., co-rulers), where they will rule over the earth for a period of a thousand years. The thousand-year period begins the second coming of Christ, after Armageddon.

**Revelation 21:4** Updated American Standard Version (UASV)

[4] and he will wipe away every tear from their eyes, and death shall be no more, neither shall there be mourning, nor crying, nor pain anymore, for the former things have passed away."

Here, we see that God links the millennium at a time when "he will wipe away every tear from their eyes, and death shall be no more, neither shall there be mourning, nor crying, nor pain anymore." Thus, it seems important that we have a correct understanding of the millennium. If we open our Bible to chapter 20, there we will discover most of what the Bible has to say about the millennium.

## Satan Bound for 1,000 Years

**Revelation 20:1-3** Updated American Standard Version (UASV)

**20** Then I saw an angel coming down from heaven, holding the key of
the abyss and a great chain in his hand. [2] And he seized the dragon, the
original serpent, who is the Devil and Satan, and bound him for a thousand
years; [3] and threw him into the abyss, and shut it and sealed it over him, so
that he might not deceive the nations any longer, until the thousand years
were ended; after these things he must be released for a short time.

Who is this angel? Robert L. Thomas offers the best insight into this question. "Various suggested identifications of the "angel" (ἄγγελον [*angelon*]) charged with the responsibility of binding Satan have been Christ, the Holy Spirit, the twelve apostles, one of the popes, and Constantine the Great.[100] None of these has convincing support, however. The better course is to understand him to be a special angel commissioned for this particular task

[100] William Lee, "The Revelation of St. John," in *The Holy Bible*, ed. F. C. Cook (London: John Murray, 1881), 4:791–92.

(Walvoord)."[101] It could not have been worded any better, "a special angel commissioned for this particular task." There are two special angels mentioned in the Bible who would have the tremendous power needed to be able to dispose of Satan.

We have **Gabriel**, the only angel other than **Michael** named in the Bible. Twice Gabriel appeared to the prophet Daniel. (Dan. 8:1, 15-26) Gabriel was tasked to bring the good news to Zechariah and Elizabeth that they would have a son, John the Baptist. (Lu 1:11-20) Gabriel also declared a special message to Mary, who was pregnant with Jesus. (Lu 1:26-38) Gabriel is a high-ranking angel who 'stands in the presence of God,' 'the angel sent from God' to deliver special messages here on earth. Gabriel is a "personal name meaning "strong man of God.""[102] Thus, Gabriel is the only *other* true candidate being sent by God to abyss Satan.

**Jude 9** Updated American Standard Version (UASV)

[9] But **Michael the archangel**, when he disputed with the devil and argued about the body of Moses, did not dare to bring a judgment against him in abusive terms, but said, "The Lord[103] rebuke you!"

Yes, the best interpretation of who this special angel might be is **Michael**. Michael is a "personal name meaning, "Who is like God?""[104] Michael is an "archangel who served as the guardian of the nation of Israel (Dan. 10:13, 21; 12:1). Together with Gabriel, Michael fought for Israel against the prince (angelic patron) of Persia. … In Rev. 12:7, Michael commands the forces of God against the forces of the dragon in a war in heaven. Jude 9 refers to a dispute between the devil and Michael over Moses' body."[105] The *Holman Illustrated Dictionary* also notes that archangel means "chief or first angel. The English term "archangel" is a derivative of the Greek word *archangelos*, which occurs only twice in the NT. Only one archangel is named in the Bible, though it is possible that there are others."[106] This author would disagree that there is any possibility that there is more than

---

[101] Robert L. Thomas, *Revelation 8-22: An Exegetical Commentary* (Chicago: Moody Publishers, 1995), 405–406.

[102] Chad Brand, Charles Draper, et al., eds., "Gabriel," *Holman Illustrated Bible Dictionary* (Nashville, TN: Holman Bible Publishers, 2003), 610.

[103] I.e., the Father; Zechariah 3:2 (UASV) Then Jehovah said to Satan, "rebuke you, Satan! Indeed, Jehovah, who has chosen Jerusalem rebuke you! Is this not a brand plucked from the fire?"

[104] Chad Brand, Charles Draper, et al., eds., "Gabriel," *Holman Illustrated Bible Dictionary* (Nashville, TN: Holman Bible Publishers, 2003), 1119.

[105] Chad Brand, Charles Draper, et al., eds., "Michael," *Holman Illustrated Bible Dictionary* (Nashville, TN: Holman Bible Publishers, 2003), 1119.

[106] John Laing, "Archangel," ed. Chad Brand et al., *Holman Illustrated Bible Dictionary* (Nashville, TN: Holman Bible Publishers, 2003), 105.

one archangel. The prefix "arch," meaning "chief" or "principal," indicates that there is only one archangel, the chief angel. Yes, Gabriel is very powerful, but no Scripture ever refers to him as an archangel. If there were multiple archangels, how could they be described as arch (chief or principal) angels? In the Scriptures, "archangel" is never found in the plural.

Clearly, Michael is the only archangel. As the highest-ranking angel, like the highest-ranking general in the army, Michael stands directly under the authority of God, as he commands the other angels, including Gabriel, according to the Father's will and purposes. This archangel, who is like God, who disputed with Satan over Moses body, who stood guard over the sons of Israel, who fought for Israel against demons, who cast Satan out of heaven, who defeated the kings of the earth and their armies at Armageddon would be the one given the privilege of abyssing Satan, the archenemy of God. – Jude 9; Daniel 10:13, 21; 12:1; Revelation 12:7-9; 18:1, 2; 19:11-21.

Michael "seized the dragon, the original serpent, who is the Devil and Satan, and bound him for a thousand years; and threw him into the abyss, and shut it and sealed it over him." The abyss could be likened to a super-maximum-security (Supermax) prison, which represents the most secure levels of custody in the prison systems, which is solitary confinement, which is used to isolate and keep the worst of the worst from having any contact with other inmates. According to *A Greek-English Lexicon of the New Testament*, the Greek abyssos means "an immensely deep space, depth, abyss."[107] On this, Kendell H. Easley writes, "The binding of the devil is triply secure: the angel **threw him into the Abyss and locked and sealed it**. The purpose is not to punish him but to **keep him from deceiving the nations anymore**. First Peter 5:8 supports the idea that the devil is reasonably free during this age: "Your enemy the devil prowls around like a roaring lion looking for someone to devour." Premillennialists believe that this binding must mean complete removal of satanic influence from the affairs of humans during the time Christ rules the nations after his return, even though there is no reference to Christ's ruling *nations* anywhere in this passage. This is the most natural reading."[108]

Even though Revelation 20:1-3 states that only Satan will be seized and thrown into the abyss prison, we can reasonably conclude that his demonic angels will also be bound and abyssed. Neither Satan nor his demon hordes will be allowed to interfere with the work of Christ and his kingdom during

[107] William Arndt, Frederick W. Danker, and Walter Bauer, *A Greek-English Lexicon of the New Testament and Other Early Christian Literature* (Chicago: University of Chicago Press, 2000), 2.

[108] Kendell H. Easley, *Revelation*, vol. 12, Holman New Testament Commentary (Nashville, TN: Broadman & Holman Publishers, 1998), 370.

the millennium. Why are Satan and his demonic angels released for a short time? At the end of Christ's thousand-year reign, humankind will have been restored to perfection, living on a paradise earth, which was the original purpose of the Father. (Gen. 1:28; 2:8, 15Isa. 45:18; Ps 104:5; 115:16; Eccl. 1:4) God did not tempt Adam with the tree of knowledge, but rather it was used as a symbol to help Adam and Eve respect God's sovereignty, his right to rule and to willingly remain under that umbrella of rule. As we know, Adam rebelled. Again, God chose a very faithful servant, Abraham, that he intended to use for his will and purpose, who would be the father of a great nation. Here again, God did not tempt Abraham with the sacrificing of his son. It was merely a means of letting Abraham see what God already knew, an evident demonstration of great faith.

Nevertheless, God allows trials to come; he does not try or tempt his servants with evil intent. What he allows is for our good, our advancement; never would he do anything that would bring us harm. God allowed Satan to tempt Job over the argument from Satan that man is only loyal to God based on what they get from him, i.e., greed, not out of love. Would Adam, Abraham, and Job see God as the rightful sovereign of the universe? after all that imperfect humanity has been through, and now that humanity has been restored to perfection, Satan and the demons are released for a little while, where humans will evidence that they recognize and willingly accept God as the rightful sovereign if the universe. (Rev. 20:3) Each one will be proved as to their integrity to God, many of which had been born during the thousand-year reign and have no experience under a Satan-ruled age that humanity had just come. (Job 1:12) Satan had induced Adam and Eve to sin, even though they were perfect. We can only assume that he will use similar tactics as before his being abyssed. Clearly, no doubt he will again appeal to selfishness, trying to convince those perfect humans that they would be better off without the rulership of God. Satan will seek to have humans rebel again. We will discuss this more below under verses 7-8.

## Millennial Rulers with Christ

**Revelation 20:4** Updated American Standard Version (UASV)

4 Then I saw thrones, and they sat on them, and judgment was given to them. And I saw the souls of those who had been beheaded[109] because of their testimony of Jesus and because of the word of God, and those who had not worshiped the beast or his image, and had not received the mark on their

---

[109] Lit *executed with the ax*

forehead and on their hand; and they came to life and reigned with Christ for a thousand years.

**Daniel 7:13-14, 18** Updated American Standard Version (UASV)

13 "I kept looking in the night visions,

and behold, with the clouds of heaven
there came one like a son of man,
and he came to the Ancient of Days
and was presented before him.
14 And to him was given dominion
and glory and a kingdom,
that all peoples, nations, and languages
should serve him;
his dominion is an everlasting dominion,
which shall not pass away,
and his kingdom one
that shall not be destroyed.

18 But the holy ones of the Most High shall receive the kingdom and possess the kingdom forever, even for ever and ever.'[110]

Who are these "holy ones" sitting on thrones and ruling in the heavens with Jesus? The "holy ones," who are to be co-rulers with Christ in his kingdom, are the elect or the chosen ones, for the sake of the chosen ones those days of the great tribulation will be cut short. (Matt. 24:21-22) They include the 12 apostles, to whom Jesus gave the promise: "in the renewal,[111] when the Son of man sits down on his glorious throne, you who have followed me will sit on twelve thrones, judging the twelve tribes of Israel." They are the "fellow heirs with Christ." (Rom. 8:17) They are pictured by the symbolic number of the twenty-four elders, clothed in white garments, with golden crowns on their heads. (Rev. 4:4) They are to be a kingdom and priests to our God, and they shall reign over the earth (Rev. 5:9-10), will reign with him for a thousand years. (Rev. 20:6) They are the ones, who will be caught up together with them in the clouds to meet the Lord in the air, and so we will always be with the Lord. (1 Thess. 4:17) Hence, Christ Jesus and these elect or chosen ones will rule the world of humankind throughout the millennium.

---

[110] Lit *and unto the age of the ages*

[111] Gr., *palingenesiai* (recreation), "an era involving the renewal of the world (with special reference to the time of the Messiah)—'new age, Messianic age.'" – GELNTSD

Who is the "son of man" referred to in Daniel 7:13-14? John F Walvoord writes, "Conservative scholars are agreed that the Son of Man is a picture of the Lord Jesus Christ rather than an angelic agency. The description of Him as being worthy of ruling all nations is obviously in keeping with many passages in the Bible referring to the millennial rule of Jesus Christ, for example, Psalm 2:6–9 and Isaiah 11. Like the scene in Revelation 4–5, Christ is portrayed as a separate person from God the Father. The expression that He is attended by "clouds of heaven" implies His deity (1 Thess. 4:17). A parallel appears in Revelation 1:7, "Behold, he is coming with the clouds," in fulfillment of Acts 1 wherein His ascension Christ was received by a cloud and the angels tell the disciples that Christ "will come in the same way as you saw him go into heaven" (Acts 1:9–11). ... Jesus' frequent use of this title for Himself in the New Testament is the divine commentary on the phrase (cf. Matt. 8:20; 9:6; 10:23; 11:19; 12:8, 32, 40; 13:37, 41; 16:13, 27, 28; 17:9, 12, 22, etc.). "Son of Man" was, in fact, Jesus' favorite description of Himself during His earthly ministry ... In verse 13, the Son of Man is presented as being near the Ancient of Days, and in verse 14 He is given dominion over all peoples and nations. This could not be an angel, nor could it be the body of saints, as it corresponds clearly to other Scriptures that predict that Christ will rule over all nations (Ps. 72:11; Rev. 19:15–16). Only Christ will come with clouds of heaven, and be the King of kings and Lord of lords over all nations throughout eternity."[112]

Clearly, among these elect or chosen ones, who are to serve as kings, priests, and judges with Christ, were some who suffered as martyrs, like Stephen before the Sanhedrin, James (son of Zebedee), James (Jesus' half-brother), the apostle Paul, Peter, Polycarp, Justin, Ignatius of Antioch, John Hus, and William Tyndale, to mention just a few. While very few of the elect or chosen ones were executed by beheading, it should be seen as an expression that may be true of a couple early apostles and simply stands for all those elect, holy ones who endure martyrdom in one way or another. The ax (Greek, *pelekus*) was apparently the customary instrument of execution in Rome: However, by the time of John writing the book of Revelation (c. 96-98 C.E.), the sword was more commonly used. *Pepelekismenon* means "to kill by beheading, normally an act of capital punishment–'to cut the head off, to behead.'"[113] (Matt. 10:22, 28) Indeed, there is little doubt that Satan would like to behead every one of the chosen ones who will serve with Christ, but

[112] John F Walvoord, *Daniel (The John Walvoord Prophecy Commentaries)* (Chicago, IL: Moody Publishers, 2012), Kindle Locations 3668-3683.

[113] Johannes P. Louw and Eugene Albert Nida, *Greek-English Lexicon of the New Testament: Based on Semantic Domains* (New York: United Bible Societies, 1996), 236–237.

not all will suffer martyrdom, as many will simply die of old age like the apostle John.

John goes on to say of these elect, chosen ones, "**they came to life and reigned with Christ for a thousand years**." Does this mean that these holy ones will not be resurrected until Michael, the archangel, has abyssed Satan and the demons? No. These ones began to be resurrected at the beginning of what is commonly called the "last days." (2 Tim. 3:1) "The 'last days' is not some future event to which we look. It is now, Jesus Christ initiated this epoch [at his ascension], and it will continue uninterrupted until his return."[114] Thus, the elect or holy ones have been and will be resurrected the moment die. In fact, these ones have been playing a role in Jesus' work all along since he ascended back to heaven. They will play a role in Armageddon.

Is this a literal thousand years? Yes, Robert L. Thomas writes, "there are many good reasons for taking one thousand to be literal (Walvoord). It is the plain statement of the text six times. [Rev. 20:3, 4, 5, 6, 7] It is doubtful that any symbolic number if there be such, is ever repeated that many times. Other symbolism in Revelation is not opposed to a literal understanding of the thousand years.[115] The mention of the thousand years is not limited to the binding of Satan. John received the information by direct revelation apart from symbols also (cf. 20:4, 5, 6) (Walvoord). Alleged problems in identifying this kingdom with the one promised in the OT—such as its limited length, rather than being eternal, and its lack of the ideal conditions cited in the OT[116]—are only apparent. The kingdom will have a limited phase and will enter its eternal phase after the conclusion of the thousand years. And it will have the ideal conditions described in the OT, but John has no occasion to mention them here."[117] Paul said that "he [God] has fixed **a day** on which he will judge the world. (Ac 17:31) Peter tells us "that with the Lord one day is like a thousand years, and a thousand years like one day." Peter's reference to a thousand years is literal. This Day of Judgment is, therefore, a literal thousand years. **Papias** (70–163 C.E.), along with **Ignatius** (c. 35–c.108 C.E.) and **Polycarp** (69–155 C.E.), was considered among the pupils of the apostle John, perhaps even his scribe. Papias later became the bishop of

---

[114] Knute Larson, *I & II Thessalonians, I & II Timothy, Titus, Philemon*, vol. 9, Holman New Testament Commentary (Nashville, TN: Broadman & Holman Publishers, 2000), 300.

[115] Contra Swete, *Apocalypse*, p. 266.

[116] Swete, *Apocalypse*, p. 264; Martin Kiddle, *The Revelation of St. John*, HNTC (New York: Harper, 1940), pp. 393–94; Johnson, "Revelation," 12:478; cf. Robert M. Johnson, "The Eschatological Sabbath in John's Apocalypse: A Reconsideration," *AUSS* 25, no. 1 (Spring 1987): 44–46; Barbara Wooten Snyder, "How Millennial Is the Millennium? A Study in the Background of the 1000 Years in Revelation 20," *Evangelical Journal* 9, no. 2 (Fall 1991): 70–72.

[117] Robert L. Thomas, *Revelation 8-22: An Exegetical Commentary* (Chicago: Moody Publishers, 1995), 409.

Hierapolis in Asia Minor. Papias believed in a literal Thousand Year Reign of Christ.

## The Beast, the Image, and the Mark

How are we to "understand those who had not worshiped the beast or his image, and had not received the mark on their forehead and on their hand"?

In our efforts to understand what is meant by the mark of the beast, the name, the number six hundred and sixty-six (666), we need to look for clues within the Scripture that will help us find the correct answer.

## The Importance of Bible Names

If anyone has read much of Scripture, they will discover that Bible names play a significant importance, especially those handed out by God himself. On this Dr. Cornwall and Smith write, "Every Bible name has a meaning. So much so, that sometimes when God changed the nature of a person He also changed his or her name. For example, when Abram believed God's promise of a son, God changed his name to Abraham ["father of a multitude"] and changed his wife's name from Sarai to Sarah ["Princess"]. Years later, after the angel of the Lord had wrestled with him all night; Jacob's name was changed to Israel ["Contender with God"]. In the New Testament, Saul of Tarsus, whose name meant "demanded," came to be known as Paul, which means "little." And this is what the greatest apostle became in his own eyes as he looked increasingly upon the greatness of Christ. It's amazing how often a Bible character lives up to the meaning of his or her name. Sometimes, as in the case of Paul, they deliberately took a name that meant what they wanted to be." (Cornwall and Smith 1998, Page viii)

We find this to be the case from Genesis to Revelation; therefore, the mark of the beast, the name, the number six hundred and sixty-six (666) given by God has to be in relation to the nature of the beast. If we are to understand the nature of the beast, we must identify the beat itself to discover what we can about its undertakings.

## The Beast Uncovered

We can actually discover much about the symbolic beast of Revelation by looking to the prophetic book of Daniel. In chapter 7 of Daniel, there are four beasts: a lion, a bear, a leopard, and "a fourth beast, terrifying and dreadful and exceedingly strong. It had great iron teeth; it devoured and broke in pieces and stamped what was left with its feet. It was different from all the beasts that were before it, and it had ten horns." (Daniel 7:2-7) If we look at verse 17 of chapter 7, Daniel tells us, "These four great beasts are four kings who shall arise out of the earth." In verse 23 of the same chapter, Daniel says, "Thus he said: 'As for the fourth beast, there shall be a fourth kingdom on earth, which shall be different from all the kingdoms, and it shall devour the whole earth, and trample it down, and break it to pieces.'" In other words, these symbolic beasts represent kingdoms that were to rule over the earth.

Regarding the beast of Revelation 13:1-2, the *Holman New Testament Commentary: Revelation* states, "The monster appears even more royal than the dragon, wearing **ten crowns** (diadems) as compared to the dragon's seven (12:3). **The blasphemous name** on each head suggests a claim to divine status (vv. 5–6). The body parts of this brute are a composite of three of the four creature of Daniel 7:1–6, but in reverse order: body of **a leopard**, feet of **a bear**, and mouth of **a lion. In** Daniel's vision, these represented historical empires that opposed Judah, such as Babylon and Persia. Here they are all combined into one monster–raw political-military power. The Christians of John's day immediately grasped that the form of the monster current in their day was imperial Rome. Where did Rome's power come from? **The dragon gave the beast his power and his throne and great authority**. Although God has ordained that government be used for good (Rom. 13:1–7), clearly the devil has mastered the art of twisting what God means for good and turning it to evil."– (Easley 1998, p. 227)

**Revelation 13:2** Updated American Standard Version (UASV)

2 And the beast which I saw was like a leopard, and his feet were like those of a bear, and his mouth like the mouth of a lion. And the dragon gave him his power and his throne and great authority.

As we saw above, these symbolic beasts represent kingdoms that were to rule over the earth. However, what do these features denote? Regarding the features of the beast of Revelation 13:1-2, the *Baker New Testament Commentary: Revelation* states, "The first portrayal is that of the leopard, noted for stalking its prey, its amazing speed in capturing prey, and its swiftness in dealing the deathblow. The second picture is that of a bear, who with its powerful paws is able to tear its victims apart. And third, the lion's mouth symbolizes cruelty as it kills and devours wild animals. The three pictures of these beasts are a depiction of force, speed, and savagery." (Kistemaker 2001, p. 379)

**Revelation 13:1** Updated American Standard Version (UASV)

[1] And the dragon stood on the sand of the sea. Then I saw a beast coming up out of the sea, having ten horns and seven heads, and on his horns were ten diadems, and on his heads were blasphemous names.

What or who do these seven heads represent? The seven heads are seven world empires throughout Bible history that have had some kind of impact on God's people, five of which were before John's day: Egypt Assyria, Babylon, Medo-Persia, and Greece. The sixth of those world empires was in existence during John's day, Rome, with the seventh world empire yet to come. Look at John's reference again in the same book.

**Revelation 17:9-10** Updated American Standard Version (UASV)

[9] Here is the mind which has wisdom. The seven heads are seven mountains on which the woman sits, **10** and they are seven kings; five have fallen **[Egypt, Assyrian, Babylon, Medo-Persia, and Greece]**, one is **[Rome]**, the other has not yet come **[?]**;and when he comes, he must remain a little while.

We can conclude that the first wild beast from the sea (vss. 1-10) and the second wild beast from the earth (vss. 11-18) of Revelation 13 represent two governmental powers. The first wild beast, "the dragon **[Satan, Rev. 12:3, 9]** gave it his power and his throne and great authority." The second wild beast "exercises all the authority of the first beast on his behalf and compels the earth and those who live on it to worship the first beast." Therefore, these beasts or governmental powers are against Christ. Consequently, they are antichrists.

We must not overreact to this, believing that everyone within the government is somehow a tool, being possessed and used by Satan or his demons. We must realize that God uses human governments for his own purposes as well. In the United States of late, we have seen what other countries have long known, without the law enforcement, a part of the government, there would be anarchy. Moreover, without the military might of the United States government, the world would be overrun by evil, such as Islam. If there were no legislatures, we would have no laws that give our human society structure. Throughout human history, some leaders and governments have been used by Satan to try and stop pure worship. Still, others have protected the rights of its citizens, including the freedom of worship. (Romans 13:3, 4; Ezra 7:11-27; Acts 13:7) Nevertheless, because of satanic influence and human imperfection, no human society has ever, nor will they ever bring true peace and security.[118]

## The Number of a Man

**Revelation 13:18** Updated American Standard Version (UASV)

18 Here is wisdom. Let the one who has understanding calculate the number of the beast, for it is the number of a man, and his number is six hundred and sixty-six.[119]

Our next clue is in the fact that the meaning of six hundred and sixty-six (666) lays in the fact that it "is the number of a man." "A man" is generic for humanity, i.e., a human number, and should not be taken as a reference to a specific man. (Luke 4:5-6; 1 John 5:19; Revelation 13:2, 18) What does the fact that it is a human number bring to the table? What do we know about humanity over the 6,000 plus years? Paul tells us, "all have sinned **[missing the mark of perfection]** and fall short of the glory of God." (Rom. 3:23) He also stated, "Sin came into the world through one man, and death through sin, and so death spread to all men because all sinned **[all are missing the mark of perfection, i.e., human imperfection]**." The world power governments mentioned above, the ones reflective in these symbolic beasts are made up of imperfect humans, names, sin, human imperfection. Jeremiah the prophet tells us why, "I know, O Jehovah, that the way of man is not in himself, that it is not in man who walks to direct his steps."–Jeremiah 10:23

## Biblical Numbers

Just as Bible names play significant importance, this is also true of numbers. For example, the number seven is often associated with what is complete or perfect. On the number seven, the *Holman Illustrated Bible Dictionary* says, "God's work of creation was both complete and perfect, and it was completed in seven days. All of mankind's existence was related to God's creative activity. The seven-day week reflected God's first creative activity. The Sabbath was that day of rest following the workweek, reflective of God's rest (Gen. 1:1–2:4). Israelites were to remember the land also and give it a sabbath, permitting it to lie fallow in the seventh year (Lev. 25:2–7).

---

[118] Because of Satan's influence over human governments, while Christians are to be in subjection to superior authorities (Rom 13:1), this is only as long as they do not ask anything that is in opposition to God's will and purpose. For example, if the government said "no more evangelizing about the Bible," we would obey God rather than man.–Acts 5:29.

[119] One early MS reads 616

Seven was also important in cultic matters beyond the Sabbath: major festivals such as Passover and Tabernacles lasted seven days as did wedding festivals (Judg. 14:12, 17). In Pharaoh's dream the seven good years followed by seven years of famine (Gen. 41:1–36) represented a complete cycle of plenty and famine. Jacob worked a complete cycle of years for Rachel; then, when he was given Leah instead, he worked an additional cycle of seven (Gen. 29:15–30). A major Hebrew word for making an oath or swearing, *shaba*, was closely related to the word 'seven,' *sheba*. The original meaning of 'swear an oath' may have been 'to declare seven times' or 'to bind oneself by seven things.' A similar use of the number seven can be seen in the NT. The seven churches (Rev. 2–3) perhaps symbolized all the churches by their number. Jesus taught that forgiveness is not to be limited, even to a full number or complete number of instances. We are to forgive, not merely seven times (already a generous number of forgiveness) but 70 times seven (limitless forgiveness, beyond keeping count) (Matt. 18:21–22). As the last example shows, multiples of seven frequently had symbolic meaning. The year of Jubilee came after the completion of every 49 years. In the year of Jubilee, all Jewish bondslaves were released, and land which had been sold reverted to its former owner (Lev. 25:8–55). Another multiple of seven used in the Bible is 70. Seventy elders are mentioned (Exod. 24:1, 9). Jesus sent out the 70 (Luke 10:1–17). Seventy years is specified as the length of the exile (Jer. 25:12, 29:10; Dan. 9:2). The messianic kingdom was to be inaugurated after a period of 70 weeks of years had passed (Dan. 9:24)." (Brand, Draper and Archie 2003, p. 1201)

Simply put, six is one short of seven. If seven represents perfection and completion, it only seems reasonable that six falls short of that. On this, *The College Press NIV Commentary: Revelation* says, "*Six* is one less than seven; it does not 'measure up' to seven or attain to the fullness of seven. Six, then, symbolizes 'incompleteness,' "imperfection," and sometimes evil." (Davis 2000, p. 21) This really ties in well with the fact that the number of the beat is a human number, being that we are under human imperfection. In short, what do we know? We know that "man" (Gk., *anthrōpos*), often signifies the whole of humankind, i.e., humanity. We also know that the number six in the Bible, one less than seven (perfect) can denote imperfection. We also know that when something is mentioned three times, it intensifies what is being said. Therefore, six hundred and sixty-six (666) could be signifying gross human imperfection.

**Revelation 20:5** Updated American Standard Version (UASV)

5 (The rest of the dead did not come to life until the thousand years were completed.) This is the first resurrection.

What is meant by the expression "come to life"? It was actually used back in Revelation 20:4, where John said, "They came to life." The "they" here is a reference to the elect, the chosen ones, who are to rule with Christ over the earth, as kings, priest and judges. Their coming to life is far faster than the expression used for the great multitude referred to in verse five, who survive Armageddon. Paul could speak of born-again Christians as being 'dead in their trespasses and sins' (Eph. 2:1), because of their inheriting Adamic sin. He also wrote, "All have sinned and fall short of the glory of God, being justified as a gift by His grace through the redemption which is in Christ Jesus. (Rom. 3:23-24, NASB) Paul told the Corinthians, "For as in Adam all die, so also in Christ all **will be made alive**." (1 Cor. 15:22, NASB) The "elect," chosen ones of Matthew 24:21-22, i.e., "the holy ones of the Most High shall receive the kingdom" spoken of in Daniel 7:18, who have been 'made a kingdom and priests,' 'to rule over the earth (Rev 5:9-10),' to 'reign with Christ for a thousand years' (Rev. 20:6), these ones were given perfect spiritual bodies. Thus, their return to perfection was immediate. However, the great multitude of other born-again Christians, who survive Armageddon, even though they are still dead in their tress passes, they will not "**not come to life until the thousand years were completed**." They will be perfect humans at that time just as Adam and Eve were prior to the rebellion in the Garden of Eden; however, with far more knowledge and experience. This section of verse 20:5 is in a parenthetical. This verse is John's brief parenthetical explanation to take pause and talk about another group of Christians other than the elect, the chosen holy ones, who had been being discussed since 20:4, and are returned to, with the closing thought of 20:5, "This is the first resurrection."

How is this, the first resurrection? As was just mentioned, John is now returning to the subject of the elect, the chosen holy ones, who are the first group of Christians that received a resurrection based on the ransom sacrifice of Jesus Christ. The resurrections in the Old Testament and those performed by Jesus and the apostle in the New Testament were not of this sort. They had purposes like evidencing the power and authority of the one performing the resurrection. All of those persons died again. "These are the ones who follow the Lamb wherever He goes. These have been purchased from among men as first fruits to God and to the Lamb." (Rev. 14:4) Moreover, these first resurrected ones are of great importance as well, as they will be co-rulers with Christ in his heavenly kingdom, judging all others that are a part of the second resurrection at the beginning of the millennium. In addition, those resurrected to a heavenly life will receive immortality, while the great multitude of Christians, who survive Armageddon, will not receive immortality but rather eternal life. Immortality (Gr, *athanasia*; deathlessness) means indestructible, "the state of not being subject to death (that which will never die)."[120] This means that Adam was not created inherently immortal, possessing deathlessness, but rather the opportunity at endless life. This is quite amazing, considering the fact that even God's angels do not possess immortality, even though they possess spirit bodies, not carnal ones. – 1 Corinthians 15:53; 1 Timothy 6:16

**Revelation 20:6** Updated American Standard Version (UASV)

6 Blessed and holy is the one who has a part in the first resurrection; over these the second death has no power, but they will be priests of God and of Christ and will reign with him for a thousand years.

What is the second death? "The lake of fire" into which death, Hades, the symbolic "wild beast" and "the false prophet," Satan, his demons, and those who live in wickedness on earth are thrown into "the second death." (Rev 20:10, 14, 15; 21:8; Matt. 25:41) Judgment day is a specific "day" (hardly ever a literal 24 hour day), when certain groups, nations, or humankind are held accountable by God. Jesus said, "The one who rejects me and does not receive my words has a judge; the word that I have spoken will judge him **on the last day**." (John 12:48) If we look at Revelation 11:17-18, we see that God begins his judging the moment that he begins ruling in a special way, i.e., after Armageddon, Jesus' kingdom of co-rulers over the earth for a millennium, the judgment day. During that thousand years reign, the elect, chosen ones, holy ones will serve as judges, priests, and rulers with Christ. In other words, the great multitude who survive Armageddon, the righteous and unrighteous who are resurrected, will be judged throughout the millennium. A thousand-year period can be viewed as a "day," for it is stated in the Bible. (2 Peter 3:8; Psalm 90:4) There is no resurrection from the second death. As we just mentioned, the elect, chosen ones, holy ones who are serving in heaven with Christ as part of his kingdom, are spirit persons and have received immortality, deathlessness, so those who are part of the first resurrection, the second death has no power. The wicked are destroyed at Armageddon, to never be resurrected again, so, the neither second death nor judgment day is applicable to them. Jesus promised the elect, "The one who conquers will not be hurt by the second death." The second death has no authority over these ones because they cannot die and have been declared righteous. They will they "will be priests of God and of Christ and will reign with him for a thousand years," judging those on earth.

---

[120] Johannes P. Louw and Eugene Albert Nida, *Greek-English Lexicon of the New Testament: Based on Semantic Domains* (New York: United Bible Societies, 1996), 267.

**Revelation 20:7** Updated American Standard Version (UASV)

[7] When the thousand years are completed, Satan will be released from his prison,

**When the thousand years are completed**, the earth will be like the Garden of Eden, a paradise earth, with all humans again living as perfect humans. This does not mean that cities and technological advancements will have been discarded. Humanity will no longer need the ransom sacrifice of Jesus Christ to cover their sins, as Adamic sin will be no more. Paul wrote, "For as in Adam all die, so also in Christ shall all be made alive. But each in his own order: Christ the firstfruits, then at his coming those who belong to Christ. **Then comes the end**, when he delivers the kingdom to God the Father after destroying every rule and every authority and power. For he must reign until he has put all his enemies under his feet. The last enemy to be destroyed is death." – 1 Corinthians 15:22-26; Romans 15:12.

Adam had the tree in the Garden of Eden, which was designed to help him evidence his willingness to see the sovereignty of God as the right way to live life and the best way to live life, i.e., the rightfulness of God's sovereignty. Abraham was asked to sacrifice his son, not knowing God was not going to actually have him go through with it, but it enabled him to evidence a faith God already knew was there. Even Jesus Christ himself was tempted in the wilderness by Satan.

**Matthew 4:1 How do we reconcile that Jesus is being led "to be" tempted by the Spirit?**

**Matthew 4:1** Updated American Standard Version (UASV)

[1] Then Jesus was led up by the Spirit into the wilderness to be tempted (Gr, *peirazo*)[121] by the devil.

The Father does **<u>not</u> tempt** us, but he does allow us to go through temptations. As we know from Adam and Abraham, the Father can **test** us, but never tempt us with sin.

The text specifically states that the Spirit led Jesus into the wilderness "to be tempted." How do we reconcile that Jesus is being led by the Spirit "to be" tempted? First, (*Peirazo*) can be rendered either as "tempted" (ESV, NIV, LEB) or "tested" (CEV, MSG), but seeing that Satan is carrying this

[121] "to obtain information to be used against a person by trying to cause someone to make a mistake, 'to try to trap, to attempt to catch in a mistake.'" – Johannes P. Louw and Eugene Albert Nida, Greek-English Lexicon of the New Testament: Based on Semantic Domains (New York: United Bible Societies, 1996), 329.

out, it is best to be rendered "tempted." This is not a literal versus a dynamic equivalent issue because almost all dynamic equivalents have "tempted."

Second, the Father would have foreknown that Satan was going to tempt Jesus and that he would wait until his weakest moment to do so. What Satan would see as an opportunity to tempt Jesus, the Father may very well see as an opportunity to test Jesus, as he did with Abraham, establishing his faithfulness, which the Father was well aware was perfectly fine. Therefore, God allowed Jesus "to be" tempted, which he used as a test to confirm what he would already know to be true, an evident demonstration of Jesus' faith. Jesus' actions would establish or demonstrate God's confidence in him. Jesus clearly revealed that his faith was a living faith. The apostle Paul wrote of Jesus, "Since he himself was tested in that which he has suffered, He is able to come to the aid of those who are tested." (Heb. 2:18) Paul wrote, "Although he [Jesus] was a son, he learned obedience from the things he he suffered. And having been made perfect, he became to all those who obey him the source of eternal salvation." – Hebrews 5:8-9.

## Satan Released, Then Destroyed

**Revelation 20:8-9** Updated American Standard Version (UASV)

8 and will come out to deceive the nations which are in the four corners of the earth, Gog and Magog, to gather them together for the war; the number of them is like the sand of the sea. 9 And they went up on the broad plain of the earth and surrounded the fortified camp of the holy ones and the beloved city, and fire came down from heaven and devoured them.

Satan is released after the thousand-year reign of Christ. Will he be successful at misleading perfect humanity yet again? He deceives "the nations which are in the four corners of the earth, Gog and Magog, to gather them together for the war." We might be baffled at who would join Satan again, after the thousands of years under his rule, followed by a thousand years of his being abyssed and humanity being under the kingdom of God. This is evidence of just how crafty and persuasive he is. He was able to mislead the perfect man Adam and millions of angels, even after they saw what happened to humans after Adam was expelled up unto the flood. (2 Peter 2:4; Jude 6) Therefore, nothing should surprise us.

The expression "four corners of the earth" does not literally mean the humans are divided amongst themselves again. It just means that those siding with Satan will separate themselves from those siding with God. Here we have one last great battle between the forces of evil and the people of God. Gog is found in chapters 38 and 39 of Ezekiel and is there applied to the leader of a storm like, multinational assault against the people of God. Magog was a land or region "in the remote parts of the north." (Eze 38:2-4, 8, 9, 13-16; 39:1-3, 6) John is using "Gog's evil forces to represent all who oppose God in the final battle in the end times under the leadership of Satan." (Knight 2003, 181)

Those who join Satan will be like, "the number of them is like the sand of the sea." These are ones who are affected by Satan's schemes, his deception. The above way of expressing it is simply to say that the number will be substantial, at least large enough that they "can surrounded the fortified camp of the holy ones and the beloved city."

"The beloved city" is the New Jerusalem, which is a heavenly city, a symbolic city, as the dimensions and splendor of New Jerusalem could not be a literal city here on earth. The New Jerusalem are those made of the elect, chosen ones, who are part of the first resurrection, who, as a bride of Christ, joined him on his throne in this symbolic city. (Rev. 21:2) The "new heavens" will rule over the "new earth," which is made up of those great multitude of Christians who survived Armageddon, those resurrected at the beginning of the millennium, and those born during the millennium. John tells us that he "saw the holy city, new Jerusalem, coming down out of heaven from God, prepared as a bride adorned for her husband." (21:2) The New Jerusalem being Christ and his kingdom heirs coming down out of heaven is their directing their attention to the holy ones here on earth coming under attack. Thomas writes, "Fire from heaven as an instrument of divine punishment is well-known (cf. Gen. 19:24; Lev. 10:2; Ezek. 38:22; 39:6; 2 Kings 1:10, 12; Luke 9:54).[122] It is a fitting climax to this last battle with Satan and his armies. The brief κατέφαγεν αὐτούς (*katephagen autous*, 'devoured them') summarizes the fate of the rebels."[123]

## The Lake of Fire and Sulfur

**Revelation 20:10** Updated American Standard Version (UASV)

**10** And the devil who deceived them was thrown into the lake of fire and brimstone, where the beast and the false prophet are also; and they will be tormented (Gr, *basanos*) day and night forever and ever.

We will deal with the lake of fire more extensively below. For now, the **lake of** fire is a symbolic place that "burns with fire and sulfur," also

[122] Ibid.; Johnson, "Revelation," 12:588.

[123] Robert L. Thomas, *Revelation 8-22: An Exegetical Commentary* (Chicago: Moody Publishers, 1995), 425–426.

described as "the second death." Unrepentant sinners, the Devil, and even death and the Grave (or, Hades) are thrown into it. The inclusion of a spirit creature and also of death and Hades, all of which cannot be affected by fire, indicates that this lake is a symbol, not of everlasting torment, but of everlasting destruction. (Rev. 19:20; 20:14, 15; 21:8) See the footnote below.[124]

The Greek word used here for "torment," *basanizo*, primarily means "to test by rubbing on the touchstone" (basanos, "a touchstone"), then, "to question by applying torture."[125] The Bible is our case law (law established on the basis of previous verdicts), which will serve as a touchstone[126] (a standard by which something is judged) that humans were never designed to walk on their own, but to live under the sovereignty of their Creator. The issues raised by Satan will have been settled by humanities walking through thousands of years of an object lesson, for which the Bible is the case law, the touchstone, which will be around forever, as a reminder of the issues raised and settled.

## The Dead Judged before the White Throne

**Revelation 20:11** Updated American Standard Version (UASV)

[11] Then I saw a great white throne and him who sat upon it, from whose presence earth and heaven fled away, and no place was found for them.

This judgment seat belongs to "God, the judge of all." (Heb. 12:23) The Father by way of the Son and his joint heirs in heaven will be judging humankind throughout the millennium. How is it that the "earth and heaven fled away"? What we have here is judgment being executed on Satan's earth and heaven.

**Revelation 20:12** Updated American Standard Version (UASV)

[12] And I saw the dead, the great and the small, standing before the throne, and scrolls were opened; and another scroll was opened, which is the book of life; and the dead were judged from the things which were written in the scrolls, according to their deeds.

---

[124] WHAT WILL HAPPEN If YOU DIE?: Should You Be Afraid of Death or of People Who Have Died? – March 6, 2018 by Edward D. Andrews (**ISBN-13** : 978-1945757839) https://www.amazon.com/dp/1945757833

[125] W. E. Vine, Merrill F. Unger, and William White Jr., Vine's Complete Expository Dictionary of Old and New Testament Words (Nashville, TN: T. Nelson, 1996), 176.

[126] A touchstone is a hard black stone formerly used to test the purity of gold and silver according to the color of the streak left when the metal was rubbed against it.

"The great and the small" encompasses the famous, well-known, important, prominent as well as the **less** famous, well-known, prestigious, prominent ones of humans that have lived and died since Adam was expelled from the Garden of Eden. On this, John wrote some two years after penning Revelation, "And he has given him authority to execute judgment because Son of Man he is. Do not marvel at this because an hour is coming when all who are in the memorial tombs will hear his voice and come out, those who have done good things to a resurrection of life, and those who have practiced evil things to the resurrection of judgment." (John 5:27-29) The apostle Paul wrote, "That there is going to be a resurrection of both the righteous and the unrighteous." (Ac 24:15) Yes, millions will receive a resurrection at the beginning of the millennium, probably gradually, so as not to overwhelm the great multitude who survived Armageddon.

"Book" is used several times figuratively in the Scriptures, as in the expressions "your [God's] book" (Ex 32:32), "book of remembrance" (Mal 3:16), and "**book of life**" (Php 4:3; Re 3:5; 20:15). It seems that all of these references are the same thing. In other words, they are a figurative book of remembrance that is used to reward "**the great and the small**" with eternal life (in heaven or on earth), if their name is written on it. If a person's name is written in the book of life, this does not mean that they were predestined to eternal life, nor that it is guaranteed to remain once there. Continued obedience and a righteous standing before God are what lead to it remaining there. "Jehovah said to Moses, Whosoever has sinned against me, him will I blot out of my book." (Ex 32:32-33) This shows that a person's name can be written in, and it can be 'blotted out,' as well as rewritten in again if he repented of his former course. – Revelation 3:5

In this section of Revelation, 20:11-15, we are dealing with the millennial reign, and it shows that the book of life is opened to receive additional names. This is because there is "a resurrection of both **the righteous** and **the unrighteous**." (Ac 24:15) The righteous are those that have a righteous standing before God, which would include the elect, the chosen ones, who received the first resurrection. In addition, the righteous would also include the great multitude, who survived the great war of Armageddon. The names of these righteous ones are already in the book of life prior to, but it is the unrighteous who are resurrected after Armageddon that is now being added to the book of life, as long as they are obedient and garner a righteous standing before God. Who are the unrighteous? These are those who never had an opportunity to hear the good news to act on it. The resurrected faithful ones, like Abraham, Moses, David, Elijah, John the Baptist, and millions of others, will also have their name already written in the book of life.

The elect, i.e., the chosen ones, who are serving with Christ as kings, priests and judges have their names *permanently* retained in "**the book of life**" (after they have faithfully died and are resurrected), as they were 'faithful until death, and God gave them the crown of life.' (John 2:10) John went on to write, "The **one who conquers** will be clothed thus in white garments, and I **will never blot his name out of the book of life**. I will confess his name before my Father and before his angels." (Rev. 3:5) For the **unrighteous**, which are resurrected and do not have their name in the book of life, if they are faithful and choose the sovereignty of God in the test of Satan at the end of the millennium, they will be written in the book of life. (Rev 20:7-8) Jesus said, "Those who have done good to the resurrection of **life**, and those who have done evil to the resurrection of **judgment**." (John 5:29, ESV) Here "life" and "judgment" are being contrasted with each other, showing that those resurrected ones "who have done evil" **after being instructed** in the inspired Scriptures and scrolls are judged to be undeserving of life. This is not about the wicked that dies before Armageddon, i.e., those who heard the biblical truth, yet continued living in sin. This would be any who turned aside from pure worship at any time during the thousand-year reign of Christ or those who reject the sovereignty of God when Satan is let loose for a little while at the end of the millennium. Their names will be blotted out of the book of life.

**Revelation 20:13** Updated American Standard Version (UASV)

13 And the sea gave up the dead which were in it, and death and Hades gave up the dead which were in them; and they were judged, every one of them according to their deeds.

**Hades.** Everyone knows that Hades was "the underground abode of the dead in Greek mythology."[127] However, as far as early Christianity, the Greek translation of the Old Testament, the Septuagint, uses the word Hades 73 times, employing it 60 times to translate the Hebrew word Sheol. Luke at Acts 2:27 write, "For you will not abandon my soul to Hades, or let your Holy One see corruption." Luke was quoting Psalm 16:10, which reads, "For you will not abandon my soul to Sheol, or let your holy one see corruption." Notice that Luke used Hades in place of Sheol. Therefore, Hades is the Greek equivalent of Sheol, as far as Christians and the Greek New Testament is concerned. In other words, Hades is also the abode of the dead in early Christian thought. Some translations choose to use a transliteration, Hades, instead of the English hell, ASV, AT, RSV, ESV, LEB, HCSB, and NASB.

---

[127] http://biblia.com/books/mwdict11/word/hades

The fire and burning within Scripture are merely representing annihilation or eternal destruction. Therefore, there is no eternal torment in Sheol (gravedom), Hades (the equivalent of Sheol) hell (English translation), Gehenna (symbol of destruction), or the lake of fire (symbol of destruction). What about the parable of the sheep (righteous) and the goats (wicked), which has the goats, or the wicked going away into eternal punishment?

**Matthew 25:46** Updated American Standard Version (UASV)

**46** And these will go away into eternal punishment [*Kolasin*],[128] but the righteous into eternal life."

*Kolasin* "akin to *kolazoo*"[129] "This means 'to cut short,' 'to lop,' 'to trim,' and figuratively a. 'to impede,' 'restrain,' and b. 'to punish,' and in the passive 'to suffer loss.'[130] The first part of the sentence is only in harmony with the second part of the sentence, if the eternal punishment is eternal death. The wicked receive eternal death and the righteous eternal life. We might at that Matthews Gospel was primarily for the Jewish Christians, and under the Mosaic Law, God would punish those who violated the law, saying they "shall be cut off [penalty of death] from Israel." (Ex 12:15; Lev 20:2-3) We need further to consider,

**2 Thessalonians 1:8-9** Updated American Standard Version (UASV)

**8** in flaming fire, inflicting vengeance on those who do not know God and on those who do not obey the gospel of our Lord Jesus. **9** These ones will pay the penalty of eternal destruction, from before the Lord[131] and from the glory of his strength,

Notice that Paul says too that the punishment for the wicked is "eternal destruction." Many times in talking with those that support the position of eternal torment in some hellfire, they will add a word to Matthew 25:46 in their paraphrase of the verse, 'eternal conscious punishment.' However, Jesus does not tell us what the eternal punishment is, just that it is a punishment, and it is eternal. Therefore, those who support eternal conscious fiery torment will read the verse to mean just that, while those, who hold the position of eternal destruction, will take Matthew 25:46 to represent that.

---

[128] That is eternal cutting off, from life. Lit., "lopping off; pruning."

[129] W. E. Vine, Merrill F. Unger, and William White Jr., Vine's Complete Expository Dictionary of Old and New Testament Words (Nashville, TN: T. Nelson, 1996), 498.

[130] Gerhard Kittel, Gerhard Friedrich, and Geoffrey William Bromiley, Theological Dictionary of the New Testament (Grand Rapids, MI: W.B. Eerdmans, 1985), 451.

[131] Lit *from before the face of the Lord*

Considering that Jesus does not define eternal punishment, this verse is not a proof text for either side of the argument.

John writes, "They were judged, every one of them according to their deeds." Again, this is not talking about the wicked that dies before Armageddon, i.e., those that heard the biblical truth yet continued to live in sin. This would be any who turned aside from pure worship at any time during the thousand-year reign of Christ or those who reject the sovereignty of God when Satan is let loose for a little while at the end of the millennium. Their names will be blotted out of the book of life.

## The End of Death and Hades

**Revelation 20:14-15** Updated American Standard Version (UASV)

14 Then death and Hades were thrown into the lake of fire. This is the second death, the lake of fire. 15 And if anyone was not found written in the book of life, he was thrown into the lake of fire.

**Lake of Fire.** A symbolic place that "burns with fire and sulfur," also described as "the second death." Unrepentant sinners, the Devil, and even death and the Grave (or Hades) are thrown into it. The inclusion of a spirit creature and of death and Hades, not all of which can be affected by fire, indicates that this lake is a symbol, not of everlasting torment, but of everlasting destruction. – Revelation 19:20; 20:14, 15; 21:8.

At the end of the millennial judgment day, "death and Hades" are now able to be destroyed. Why was death and Hades not removed right after Armageddon? This is because some will be destroyed during the millennium, and many will be destroyed after Satan is let loose for a little while.

**1 Corinthians 15:23-28** Updated American Standard Version (UASV)

23 But each in his own order: Christ the first fruits, afterward those who belong to the Christ at his coming,[132] 24 then comes the end, when he hands over the kingdom to the God and Father, when he has abolished all rule and all authority and power. 25 For he must reign until he has put all his enemies under his feet. 26 The last enemy that will be abolished is death. 27 For he put all things in subjection under his feet. But when he says, "All things are put in subjection," it is evident that he is excepted who put all things in subjection to him. 28 When all things are subjected to him, then the Son himself also will

---

[132] Or *presence* (Gr *parousia*), which denotes both an "arrival" and a consequent "presence with."

be subjected to the One who subjected all things to him, so that God may be all in all.

**15:23.** Having given a theological justification for calling Christ the firstfruits, Paul continued the analogy. The term *firstfruits* suggests a certain order. Resurrection will happen **to each in his own turn**. First, **Christ** as the **firstfruits** has already been resurrected. Second, **those who belong to him**—those who have exercised saving faith in Christ—will be raised along with Christ. This second resurrection will occur **when he comes** in the second advent. Thus far, Paul had not taken the analogy of firstfruits beyond his discussion in the preceding verses. But at this point, he turned to an additional dimension of the analogy.

**15:24.** After Christ returns, **then the end will come**. It will be time for the final judgment and the formation of the new creation. At this time, Christ will give **over the kingdom to God the Father**. Just as the firstfruits of the Old Testament sacrificial system were symbolic of the giving over of an entire harvest to God, Christ's resurrection was symbolic of a much greater harvest to be given to God the Father—the harvest of the entire kingdom. Just as an entire harvest exceeds the firstfruits, so the harvest of the dominion given to the Father will be beyond measure.

This handing over to the Father will occur only after Christ **has destroyed all dominion, authority and power**. Elsewhere Paul used this terminology to describe both human authority (Rom. 13:1–3) and demonic powers (Eph. 1:21). In this context he had in mind the destruction of all powers that are raised against the kingdom of Christ, whether human or supernatural.

**15:25.** Paul had just set forth a complex scenario that pointed to Christ as the firstfruits: Christ's resurrection, then believers' resurrection, then the destruction of authorities and the deliverance of the kingdom to the Father. To explain this scenario further, Paul pointed out that Christ **must reign until he has put all his enemies under his feet**. This verse recalls Psalm 110:1. This psalm spoke of the promise of great victories given to the descendants of David. Every time a Davidic king experienced victory over an enemy, he saw this dynastic promise realized in his life. Paul applied this psalm to Christ, since Christ is the great and final son to sit on David's throne (Mark 11:10). In Christ all the promises to David's family come to full realization.

Paul focused here on reigning in victory. The New Testament explains that Christ was seated on the throne of David at the time of his resurrection and ascension (Eph. 1:20–21). God once promised that

David's family would rule over the entire earth (Ps. 89:20–29), and this promise now applies to Christ. Thus, it is necessary that Christ eventually reign over everyone and everything.

**15:26–27a.** Of course, **the last enemy** that Christ will destroy is **death** itself. Adam introduced death into the human race (Rom. 5:12–14), but Christ has come to eliminate death. Yet, this destruction of death will take place gradually. The elimination of death is the last great work of Christ. This will occur when he raises believers to everlasting life and frees them from the power of death (Heb. 2:14–15).

How can we know death will be destroyed? Paul referred once again to Psalm 110:1, emphasizing that Christ would dominate everything. He considered it an indisputable fact that the great son of David would reign over all things, including death itself. Since Christ would reign over death, those in Christ would not be subjected to death's dominion. For this reason, the general resurrection of all believers is a certainty.

**15:27b–28.** Realizing that he had pushed the term *everything* to the limits, Paul qualified himself to avoid confusion. He noted that it was **clear** or obvious to those reading Psalm 110 that the term *everything* did **not include God himself**, because God the Father is the one **who put everything under Christ**. In other words, Psalm 110:1 makes it plain that God puts everything under the feet of David's son. For this reason, the Father remains superior to the Christ. As a result, when all is accomplished **the Son himself will be made subject** to the Father. In perfect harmony with the idea of Christ as the firstfruits that honor God as the one who gives harvest, Christ will remain in subjection to the Father **so that God may be all in all.**[133]

133 Richard L. Pratt Jr, *I & II Corinthians*, vol. 7, Holman New Testament Commentary (Nashville, TN: Broadman & Holman Publishers, 2000), 264–265.

# APPENDIX C Authorship of Daniel Defended

## Daniel Misjudged

You have a critical body that has formulated an opinion of the Bible, especially prophetic books, long before they have ever looked into the evidence. The liberal critical scholar is antisupernatural in their mindset. In other words, any book that would claim to have predicted events hundreds of years in advance are simply misrepresenting itself, as that foreknowledge is impossible. Therefore, the book must have been written after the events, yet written in such a way, as to mislead the reader that it was written hundreds of years before.

This is exactly what these critics say we have in the book of Daniel. However, what do we know about the person and the book itself? Daniel is known historically as a man of uprightness in the extreme. The book that he penned has been regarded highly for thousands of years. The context says that it is authentic and true history, penned by Daniel, a Jewish prophet, who lived in the seventh and sixth centuries. The chronology within the book shows that it covers the time period of 616 to 536 B.C.E., being completed by the latter date.

*The New Encyclopædia Britannica* acknowledges that the book of Daniel was once "generally considered to be true history, containing genuine prophecy." However, the *Britannica* asserts that in truth, Daniel "was written in a later time of national crisis—when the Jews were suffering severe persecution under [Syrian King] Antiochus IV Epiphanes." This encyclopedia dates the book between 167 and 164 B.C.E. *Britannica* goes on to assert that the writer of the book of Daniel does not prophesy the future but merely presents "events that are past history to him as prophecies of future happenings."

How does a book and a prophet that has enjoyed centuries of a reputable standing, garner such criticism? It actually began just two-hundred years after Christ, with Porphyry, a philosopher, who felt threatened by the rise of Christianity. His way of dealing with this new religion was to pen fifteen books to undercut it, the twelfth being against Daniel. In the end, Porphyry labeled the book as a forgery, saying that it was written by a second-century B.C.E. Jew. Similar attacks came in the 18th and 19th centuries. German scholars, who were prejudiced against the supernatural, started modern objections to the Book of Daniel.

As has been stated numerous times in this section, the higher critics and rationalists start with the presupposition that foreknowledge of future events is impossible. As was stated earlier in the chapter on Isaiah, the **important truth for the Bible critic is** the understanding that in all occurrences, prophecy pronounced or written in Bible times meant something to the people of the time it was spoken or written to; it was meant to serve as a guide for them. Frequently, it had specific fulfillment for that time, being fulfilled throughout the lifetime of that very generation. This is actually true; the words always had some application to the very people who heard them. However, the application could be a process of events, starting with the moral condition of the people in their relationship with Jehovah God, which precipitated the prophetic events that were to unfold, even those prophetic events that were centuries away.

However, it must be noted that while Daniel and Isaiah are both prophetic books, Daniel is also known as an apocalyptic book, as is the book of Revelation. This is not to say that Isaiah does not contain some apocalyptic sections (e.g., Isa 24–27; 56–66) What is assumed by the critical scholar here is that there is a rule that a prophet is understood in his day, to be only speaking of the immediate concerns of the people. They are looking at it more like a proclamation, instead of a future event that could be centuries away. Before addressing this concern, let us define apocalyptic for the reader:

## Apocalyptic

This is a term derived from a Greek word meaning "revelation," and used to refer to a pattern of thought and to a form of literature, both dealing with future judgment (eschatology).

Two primary patterns of eschatological thought are found in the Bible, both centered in the conviction that God will act in the near future to save his people and to punish those who oppress them. In prophetic eschatology, the dominant form in the OT, God is expected to act within history to restore man and nature to the perfect condition which existed prior to man's fall. Apocalyptic eschatology, on the other hand, expects God to destroy the old imperfect order before restoring the world to paradise.

## Origins of Apocalypticism

In Israel, apocalyptic eschatology evidently flourished under foreign domination.

> From the early 6th century B.C., prophetic eschatology began to decline and apocalyptic eschatology became increasingly popular. The Book of Daniel, written during the 6th-century B.C., is the earliest example of apocalyptic literature in existence.[134]

The problem with the modern critic is that he is attempting to look at the Biblical literature through the modern-day mindset. His first error is to believe that a prophetic book was viewed only as a proclamation of current affairs. The Jewish people viewed all prophetic literature just as we would expect, as a book of prophecy. The problem today is that many are not aware of the way they viewed the prophetic literature. While we do not have the space to go into the genre of prophecy and apocalyptic literature extensively, it is recommended that you see Dr. Stein's book in the bibliography at the end of the chapter.

## Some Rules for Prophecy

- One needs to identify the beginning and end of the prophecy.
- The reader needs to find the historical setting.
- The Bible is a diverse book when it comes to literary styles: narrative, poetic, prophetic, and apocalyptic; also containing parables, metaphors, similes, hyperbole, and other figures of speech. Too often, these alleged errors are the result of a reader taking a figure of speech as literal or reading a parable as though it is a narrative.
- Many alleged inconsistencies disappear by simply looking at the context. Taking words out of context can distort their meaning.
- Determine if the prophet is foretelling the future. (If prophetic, has any portion of it been fulfilled?) on the other hand, is he simply proclaiming God's will and purpose to the people.
- The concept of a second fulfillment should be set aside in place of implications.
- Does the New Testament expound on this prophecy?
- The reader needs to slow down and carefully read the account, considering exactly what is being said.

---

[134] Walter A. Elwell and Barry J. Beitzel, *Baker Encyclopedia of the Bible* (Grand Rapids, Mich.: Baker Book House, 1988), 122.

- The Bible student needs to understand the level that the Bible intends to be exact in what is written. If Jim told a friend that 650 graduated with him from high school in 1984, it is not challenged, because it is all too clear that he is using rounded numbers and is not meaning to be exactly precise.
- Unexplained does not become unexplainable.

Digging into the ancient Jewish mindset, we find that it is dualistic. It views all of God's creation, either on the side of God or Satan. Further, the Jewish mind was determined that regardless of how bad things were, God would come to rescue his people. The only pessimistic thinking was their understanding that there had to be a major catastrophe that precipitated the rescue. In combining this way of thinking, they believed that there are two systems of things: (1) the current wicked one that man lives in, and (2) the one that is to come, where God will restore things to the way it was before Adam and Eve sinned. Jehovah impressed upon his people to see His rescue as imminent. The vision that comes to Daniel in the book of Daniel and John in Revelations comes in one of two ways: (1) in a dreamed vision state or (2) the person in vision is caught up to heaven and shown what is to take place. Isaiah, Daniel and John frequently did not understand the vision; they were simply to pen what they saw. (Isa 6:9-10; 8:16; 29:9-14; 44:18; 53:1; Dan 8:15–26; 9:20–27; 10:18–12:4; Rev 7:13–17; 17:7–18) The people readily recognized the symbolism in most of the prophetic literature, and the less common symbolisms in apocalyptic literature were far more complex, which by design, heighten the desire to interpret and understand them. There are two very important points to keep in mind: (1) some were not meant to be understood fully at the time, and (2) only the righteous ones would have insight into these books, while the wicked would refuse to understand the spiritual things.

**Daniel 8:26-27** Updated American Standard Version (UASV)

26 The vision of the evenings and the mornings that has been told is true,[135] but seal up the vision,[136] for it refers to many days from now."[137]

27 And I, Daniel, was exhausted and sick for days. Then I got up and carried out the business of the king, and I was disturbed over the vision and no one could understand it.[138]

---

135 Lit *truth*; Heb., *'emet*

136 I.e., keep the vision secret; Heb., *satar*

137 Lit *for to days many*; I.e., to the distant future

138 Lit *make* me *understand*

**Daniel 10:14** Updated American Standard Version (UASV)

14 Now I have come to give you an understanding of what will happen to your people in the end of the days, for it is a vision yet for the days to come."

**Daniel 12:3-4** Updated American Standard Version (UASV)

3 And the ones who are wise will shine brightly like the brightness of the expanse of heaven; and those who turn many to righteousness, like the stars forever and ever. 4 But as for you, O Daniel, conceal these words and seal up the book until the time of the end; many will go to and fro,[139] and knowledge will increase."

**Daniel 12:9-10** Updated American Standard Version (UASV)

9He said, "Go your way, Daniel, for the words are shut up and sealed until the time of the end. 10Many shall purify themselves and make themselves white and be refined, but the wicked shall act wickedly. And none of the wicked shall understand, but those who are wise shall understand.

**2 Corinthians 4:3-4** Updated American Standard Version (UASV)

3 And even if our gospel is veiled, it is veiled to those who are perishing. 4 In their case the god of this world has blinded the minds of the unbelievers, to keep them from seeing the light of the gospel of the glory of Christ, who is the image of God.

One of the principles of interpreting prophecy is to understand judgment prophecies. If a prophet declares judgment on a people and turns around from their wrong course, the judgment may be lifted, which does not negate the trueness of the prophetic judgment message. There was simply a change in circumstances. There is a principle that most readers are not aware of:

**Jeremiah 18:7-8** Updated American Standard Version (UASV)

7 At one moment I might speak concerning a nation or concerning a kingdom to uproot, to tear down, and to destroy it; 8 and if that nation which I have spoken against turns from its evil, I will also feel regret over[140] the calamity that I intended to bring against it.

---

139 That is, examine the book thoroughly

140 Lit *repent of*; .e., *I will change my mind concerning*; or *I will think better of*, or *I will relent concerning*

Another principle that needs to be understood is the language of prophecy. It uses imagery that is common to the people, with the exception of the highly apocalyptic literature. One form of imagery is cosmic.

**Isaiah 13:9-11** Updated American Standard Version (UASV)

9 Behold, the day of Jehovah is coming,
cruel, with wrath and burning anger,
to make the land a desolation;
and he will destroy its sinners from it.
10 For the stars of the heavens and their constellations
will not flash forth their light;
the sun will be dark when it rises,
and the moon will not shed its light.
11 And I will punish the world for its evil,
and the wicked for their iniquity;
I will put an end to the arrogance of the proud,
and lay low the haughtiness of tyrants.

It is often assumed that this imagery is about the end of the world, and this is not always the case. Using Isaiah 13 as our example, it is talking about a pronouncement against Babylon, not the end of the world, as can be seen in verse 1. This type of terminology is a way of expressing that God is acting on behalf of man. At times, figurative language can come across as contradicting for the modern-day reader. For example, in chapter 21 of Revelation the walls of Jerusalem are described as being 200 feet thick. The walls are an image of safety and security for the New Jerusalem. However, in verse 25 we read that the gates are never shut. This immediately leads to the question of why have walls that cannot be penetrated and then leave the gates open? Moreover, if gates are the weakest point to defend, why have twelve of them (vs. 12)? This comes off as contradictory to the modern militaristic mind, but not to the Jewish-Christian mind of the first-century. Both present the picture of safety. It is so safe that you can leave the gates open. What about the idea of a "fuller meaning" that the prophet was not aware of? As we saw in the above, there would be symbolism meant for a day far into the future, but generally speaking, most prophets proclaimed a message that was applicable to their day and implications for another day. Dr. Robert Stein addresses this issue:

> There are times when a prophetic text appears to have a fulfillment other than what the prophet himself apparently expected. (The following are frequently given as examples: Matt. 1:22–23; 2:15, 17–18; John 12:15; 1 Cor. 10:3–4.) Is it possible that a prophecy may have a deeper meaning or "fuller" sense than the

> prophet envisioned? . . . Rather than appealing to a "fuller sense" distinct and different from that of the biblical author, however, it may be wiser to see if the supposed sensus plenior is in reality an implication of the author's conscious meaning. Thus, when Paul in 1 Corinthians 9:9 quotes Deuteronomy 25:4 ("do not muzzle an ox while it is treading out the grain") as a justification for ministers of the gospel living off the gospel, this is not a "fuller" meaning of the text unrelated to what the author sought to convey. Rather, it is a legitimate implication of the willed pattern of meaning contained in Deuteronomy 25:4. If as a principle animals should be allowed to share in the benefits of their work, how much more should the "animal" who is made in the image of God and proclaims the Word of God be allowed to share in the benefits of that work! Thus, what Paul is saying is not a fuller and different meaning from what the writer of Deuteronomy meant. On the contrary, although this specific implication was unknown to him, it is part of his conscious and willed pattern of meaning. Perhaps such prophecies as Matthew 1:22–23 and 2:15 are best understood as revealing implications of the original prophecies in Isaiah 7:14 and Hosea 11:1. Whereas in Isaiah's day the prophet meant that a maiden would give birth to a son who was named "Immanuel," that willed meaning also allows for a virgin one day to give birth to a son who would be Immanuel. Whereas God showed his covenantal faithfulness by leading his "son," his children, back from Egypt to the promised land in Moses' day so also did he lead his "Son," Jesus, back from Egypt to the promised land. [141]

Getting back to Daniel, we can clearly see that his book is prophetic and the only Old Testament apocalyptic book at that, which makes him a special target for the Bible critic. The critic has deemed that Daniel did not pen the book that bears his name, but another writer penned the words some centuries later.[142] These attacks have become such a reality that most scholars accept the late date of 165 B.C.E. by a pseudonym. As we have learned throughout this book, it is never the majority that establishes something as being true, simply for the fact of being the majority; it is the evidence. If the

---

[141] Robert H. Stein, *A Basic Guide to Interpreting the Bible: Playing by the Rules* (Grand Rapids, MI: Baker Books, 1994), 97.

[142] Some Bible critics attempt to lessen the charge of forgery by saying that the writer used Daniel as a false name (pseudonym), just as some ancient noncanonical books were written under assumed names. In spite of this, the Bible critic Ferdinand Hitzig held: "The case of the book of Daniel, if it is assigned to any other [writer], is different. Then it becomes a forged writing, and the intention was to deceive his immediate readers, though for their good."

evidence proves that Daniel did not write the book, then the words are meaningless, and the hope that it contains is not there.

For example, take the allegation made in *The Encyclopedia Americana:* "Many historical details of the earlier periods [such as that of the Babylonian exile] have been badly garbled" in Daniel. Really? We will take up three of those alleged mistakes.

## Claims That Belshazzar Is Missing from History

**Daniel 5:1, 11, 18, 22, 30** Updated American Standard Version (UASV)

1 Belshazzar the king made[143] a great feast for a thousand of his nobles, and he was drinking wine in the presence of the thousand.

11 There is a man in your kingdom in whom is a spirit of the holy gods;[144] and in the days of your father, enlightenment, insight and wisdom like the wisdom of the gods were found in him. And King Nebuchadnezzar, your father, your father the king, appointed him chief of the magic-practicing priests, conjurers, Chaldeans and diviners.

18 You. O king, the Most High God granted the kingdom and the greatness and the glory and the majesty to Nebuchadnezzar your father.

22 "But you, his son[145] Belshazzar, have not humbled your heart, although you knew all of this,

30 That same night Belshazzar the Chaldean king was killed.

In 1850 German scholar Ferdinand Hitzig said in a commentary on the book of Daniel, confidently declaring that Belshazzar was "a figment of the writer's imagination."[146] His reasoning was that Daniel was missing from history, only found in the book of Daniel itself. Does this not seem a bit premature? Is it so irrational to think that a person might not be readily located by archaeology, a brand new field at the time, especially from a period that was yet to be fully explored? Regardless, in 1854, there was a discovery of some small cylinders in the ancient city of Babylon and Ur, southern Iraq. The cuneiform documents were from King Nabonidus, and they included a

143 I.e., held

144 Spirit of … gods Aram., *ruach-'elahin';* Or possibly *the Spirit of the holy God*

145 Or *descendant*

146 *Das Buch Daniel.* Ferdinand Hitzig. Weidman (Leipzig) 1850.

prayer for "Belshazzar my firstborn son, the offspring of my heart." This discovery was a mere four years after Hitzig made his rash judgment.

Of course, not all critics would be satisfied. H. F. Talbot made the statement, "This proves nothing." The charge by Talbot was that Belshazzar was likely a mere child, but Daniel has him as being king. Well, this critical remark did not even stay alive as long as Hitzig's had. Within the year, more cuneiform tablets were discovered. This time they stated he had secretaries, as well as household staff. Obviously, Belshazzar was not a child! However, more was to come, as other tablets explained that Belshazzar was a coregent king while Nabonidus was away from Babylon for years at a time.[147]

One would think that the critic might concede. Still disgruntled, some argued that the Bible calls Belshazzar the son of Nebuchadnezzar and not the son of Nabonidus. Others comment that Daniel nowhere mentions the name of Nabonidus. Once again, both arguments are dismantled with a deeper observation. Nabonidus married the daughter of Nebuchadnezzar, making Belshazzar the grandson of Nebuchadnezzar. Both Hebrew and Aramaic language do not have words for "grandfather" or "grandson"; "son of" also means "grandson of" or even "descendant of." (See Matthew 1:1.) Moreover, the account in Daniel does infer that Belshazzar is the son of Nabonidus. When the mysterious handwriting was on the wall, the horrified Belshazzar offered the *third* place in his kingdom to whoever could interpret it. (Daniel 5:7) The observant reader will notice that Nabonidus held first place in the kingdom, while Daniel held the second place, leaving the third place for the interpreter.

## Darius the Mede

One would think that the critic would have learned his lesson from Belshazzar. However, this is just not the case. Daniel 5:31 reads: "Darius the Mede received the kingdom, about sixty-two years old." The critical scholar again argues that Darius does not exist, as he has never been found in secular or archaeological records. Therefore, *The New Encyclopædia Britannica* declares that this Darius is "a fictitious character."

There is no doubt that Darius will be unearthed by archaeology in time, just as Belshazzar has. There is initial information that allows for inferences already. Cuneiform tablets have been discovered that show Cyrus the Persian

[147] When Babylon fell, Nabonidus was away. Therefore, Daniel was correct in that Belshazzar was the king at that time. Critics still try to cling to their Bible difficulty by stating that no secular records state that Belshazzar was a king. When will they quit with this quibbling? Even governors in the Ancient Near East were stated as being kings at times.

did not take over as the "King of Babylon" directly after the conquest. Rather he carried the title "King of the Lands."[148] W. H Shea suggests, "Whoever bore the title of 'King of Babylon' was a vassal king under Cyrus, not Cyrus himself." Is it possible that Darius is simply a title of a person that was placed in charge of Babylon? Some scholars suggest a man named Gubaru was the real Darius. Secular records do show that Cyrus appointed Gubaru as governor over Babylon, giving him considerable power. Looking to the cuneiform tablets again, we find that Cyrus appointed subgovernors over Babylon. Fascinatingly, Daniel notes that Darius selected 120 satraps to oversee the kingdom of Babylon. – Daniel 6:1.

We should realize that archaeology is continuously bringing unknown people to light all the time, and in time, it may shed more light on Darius. However, for now, and based on the fact that many Bible characters have been established, it is a little ridiculous to consider Darius as "fictitious," worse still to view the whole of the book of Daniel as a fraud. In fact, it is best to see Daniel as a person, who was right there in the midst of that history, giving him access to more court records.

After Belshazzar (King of Babylon), Sargon (Assyrian Monarch), and the like have been assailed with being nonexistent, the Bible critic and liberal scholars do the same with Darius the Mede and Mordecai in the book of Esther. This illustrates the folly of assigning boundless confidence in the ancient secular records while we wait in secular sources to validate Scripture. Most outside of true conservative Christianity carries the presupposition that much of the Bible is a myth, legend, and erroneous until secular authorities support it.

Bible critics argued profusely that Belshazzar was not a historical person. Then, evidence came in that substantiated Belshazzar. The Bible critic just moves on to another like Sargon, saying that he was not a real historical person, as though they had never raised such an objection Belshazzar. Then, evidence came in that substantiated Sargon and the Bible critic would silently move on yet again. This is repeated time after time.

The Bible critics, liberal and moderate Bible scholars believe the Bible is wrong until validated by secular history. They move the goal post of trustworthiness as they please so that Scripture will never be authentic and true, it will never be trustworthy, and to these ones, it is not the inspired, fully inerrant Word of God, as far as they are concerned.

---

[148] This evidence is found in royal titles in economic texts, which just so happens to date to the first two years of Cyrus' rule.

Why do we continue to cater to these ones, as though we need to appease them somehow?

## King Jehoiakim

**Daniel 1:1** Updated American Standard Version (UASV)

1 In the third year of the reign of Jehoiakim king of Judah, Nebuchadnezzar king of Babylon came to Jerusalem and besieged it.

**Jeremiah 25:1** Updated American Standard Version (UASV)

1 The word that came to Jeremiah concerning all the people of Judah, in the fourth year of Jehoiakim the son of Josiah, king of Judah (that was the first year of Nebuchadnezzar king of Babylon),

**Jeremiah 46:2** Updated American Standard Version (UASV)

2 About Egypt, concerning the army of Pharaoh Neco king of Egypt, which was by the Euphrates River at Carchemish, which Nebuchadnezzar king of Babylon defeated in the fourth year of Jehoiakim the son of Josiah, king of Judah:

The Bible critic finds fault with Daniel 1:1 as it is not in harmony with Jeremiah, who says, "in the fourth year of Jehoiakim the son of Josiah, king of Judah (that was the first year of Nebuchadnezzar king of Babylon)." The Bible student who looks a little deeper will find that there is really no contradiction at all. Pharaoh Necho first made Jehoiakim king in 628 B.C.E. Three years would pass before Nebuchadnezzar succeeded his father as King in Babylon in 624 B.C.E. In 620 B.C.E., Nebuchadnezzar conquered Judah and made Jehoiakim the subordinate king under Babylon. (2 Kings 23:34; 24:1) Therefore, it is all about the perspective of the writer and where he was when penning his book. Daniel wrote from Babylon; therefore, Jehoiakim's third year would have been when he was made a subordinate king to Babylon. On the other hand, Jeremiah wrote from Jerusalem, so he is referring to the time when Jehoiakim was made a subordinate king under Pharaoh Necho.

This so-called discrepancy just adds more weight to the fact that Daniel penned the book bearing his name. In addition, it must be remembered that Daniel had Jeremiah's book with him. (Daniel 9:2) Therefore, are we to believe that Daniel was this clever forger, and at the same time, he would contradict the well-known book of Jeremiah, especially in verse 1?

## Positive Details

There are many details in the book of Daniel itself, which give credence to its authenticity. For example, Daniel 3:1-6 tells us that Nebuchadnezzar set up a huge image of gold, which his people were to worship. Archaeology has found evidence that credits Nebuchadnezzar with attempts to involve the people more in nationalistic and religious practices. Likewise, Daniel addresses Nebuchadnezzar's arrogant attitude about his many construction plans. (Daniel 4:30) It was not until modern-day archaeology uncovered evidence that we now know Nebuchadnezzar was the person who built much of Babylon. Moreover, his boastful attitude is made quite evident by having his name stamped on the bricks. This fact would not have been something a forger from 167-63 B.C.E. would have known about because the bricks hadn't at that time been unearthed.

The writer of Daniel was very familiar with the differences between Babylonian and Medo-Persian law. The three friends of Daniel were thrown into the fiery furnace for disobeying the Babylonian law. In contrast, decades later under Persian law, Daniel was thrown into a lion's pit for violating the law. (Daniel 3:6; 6:7-9) Archaeology has again proven to be a great help, for they have uncovered an actual letter that shows the fiery furnace was a form of punishment. However, the Medes and Persians would have not used this form of punishment as fire was sacred to them. Thus, they had other forms of capital punishment.

Another piece of inside knowledge is that Nebuchadnezzar passed and changed laws as he pleased. On the other hand, Darius was unable to change a law once it was passed, even one that he himself had commissioned. (Daniel 2:5, 6, 24, 46-49; 3:10, 11, 29; 6:12-16) Historian John C. Whitcomb writes: "Ancient history substantiates this difference between Babylon, where the law was subject to the king, and Medo-Persia, where the king was subject to the law."

**Daniel 5:1-4** Updated American Standard Version (UASV)

1 Belshazzar the king made[149] a great feast for a thousand of his nobles, and he was drinking wine in the presence of the thousand.

2 Belshazzar, when he tasted the wine, commanded that the vessels of gold and of silver that Nebuchadnezzar his father[150] had taken out of the temple in Jerusalem be brought, that the king and his nobles, his wives, and

[149] I.e., held

[150] Or *predecessor*; also verses 11, 13, 18

his concubines might drink from them. [3] Then they brought the gold vessels that had been taken out of the temple, the house of God which was in Jerusalem; and the king and his nobles, his wives and his concubines drank from them. [4] They drank the wine and praised the gods of gold and silver, of bronze, iron, wood and stone.

Archaeology has substantiated these kinds of feasts. The fact that stands out is the mention of women being present at the feast, the "wives, and his concubines" were present as well. Such an idea would have been repugnant to the Greeks and Jews of the 167-67 B.C.E. era. This may very well be why the Greek Septuagint version of Daniel removed the mention of these women.[151] This so-called forger of Daniel would have lived during this same time of the Septuagint.

## Do External Factors Prove Daniel Is A Forgery?

Even the place of Daniel in the canon of the Hebrew Old Testament is evidence against his having written the book, so says the critics. The Jewish scribes (like Ezra) of ancient Israel arranged the books of the Old Testament into three groups: the Torah, the Prophets, and the Writings. Naturally, we would expect that Daniel would be found among the Prophets, yet they placed him among the Writings. Therefore, the critic argues that Daniel had to have been an unknown when the works of the prophets were being collected. Their theory is that it was placed among the writings because these were collected last.

However, not all Bible scholars agree that the ancient scribes placed Daniel in the Writings, and not the Prophets. However, even if it is as they claim, Daniel was added among the Writings; this does nothing to prove that it was penned at a later date. Old Testament Bible scholar Gleason L. Archer states that . . .

> It should be noted that some of the documents in the Kethubhim [Writings] (the third division of the Hebrew Bible) were of great antiquity, such as the book of Job, the Davidic psalms, and the writings of Solomon. Position in the Kethubhim, therefore, is no proof of a late date of composition. Furthermore the statement in Josephus (Contra Apionem. 1:8) quoted previously in chapter 5 indicates strongly that in the first century A.D., Daniel was included among the prophets in the second

---

[151] Hebrew scholar C. F. Keil writes of Daniel 5:3: "The LXX. have here, and also at ver. 23, omitted mention of the women, according to the custom of the Macedonians, Greeks, and Romans."

division of the Old Testament canon; hence it could not have been assigned to the Kethubim until a later period. 349 The Masoretes may have been influenced in this reassignment by the consideration that Daniel was not appointed or ordained as a prophet but remained a civil servant under the prevailing government throughout his entire career. Second, a large percentage of his writings does not bear the character of prophecy, but rather of history (chaps. 1-6), such as does not appear in any of the books of the canonical prophets.350 Little of that which Daniel wrote is couched in the form of a message from God to His people relayed through the mouth of His spokesman. Rather, the predominating element consists of prophetic visions granted personally to the author and interpreted to him by angels.[152]

The critic also turns his attention to the Apocryphal book, Ecclesiasticus, by Jesus Ben Sirach, penned about 180 B.C.E., as evidence that Daniel did not pen the book that bears his name. Ecclesiasticus has a long list of righteous men, of which, Daniel is missing. From this, they conclude that Daniel had to of been an unknown at the time. However, if we follow that line of reasoning; what do we do with the fact that the same list omits: Ezra and Mordecai, good King Jehoshaphat, and the upright man Job; of all the judges, except Samuel.[153] Simply because the above faithful and righteous men are missing from a list in an apocryphal book, are we to dismiss them as having never existed? The very idea is absurd.

## Sources in Favor of Daniel

Ezekiel's references to Daniel must be considered to be one of the strongest arguments for a sixth-century date. No satisfactory explanation exists for the use of the name Daniel by the prophet Ezekiel other than that he and Daniel were contemporaries and that Daniel had already become widely known throughout the Babylonian Empire by the time of Ezekiel's ministry.[154]

---

152 Archer, Gleason (1996-08-01). A Survey of Old Testament Introduction (Kindle Locations 7963-7972). Moody Publishers.

153 If we turn our attention to the Apostle Paul's list of faithful men and women found in Hebrews chapter 11; it does appear to mention occasions recorded in Daniel. (Daniel 6:16-24; Hebrews 11:32, 33) Nevertheless, the list by Paul is not an exhaustive list either. Even within his list, Isaiah, Jeremiah, and Ezekiel are not named in the list, but this scarcely demonstrates that they never existed.

154 Stephen R. Miller, vol. 18, *Daniel*, electronic ed., Logos Library System; The New American Commentary (Nashville: Broadman & Holman Publishers, 2001), 42-43.

> We have in chapter 9 a series of remarkable predictions which defy any other interpretation but that they point to the coming of Christ and His crucifixion [about] a.d. 30, followed by the destruction of the city of Jerusalem within the ensuing decades. In Dan. 9:25–26, it is stated that sixty-nine heptads of years (i.e., 483 years) will ensue between a "decree" to rebuild the walls of Jerusalem, and the cutting off of Messiah the Prince. In 9:25–26, we read: "Know therefore and understand, that from the going forth of the commandment to restore and to build Jerusalem unto the Messiah the Prince shall be seven weeks, and threescore and two weeks.… And after threescore and two weeks shall Messiah be cut off, but not for himself: and the people of the prince that shall come shall destroy the city and the sanctuary."[155]

## The Greatest Evidence for Daniel

> First of all, we have the clear testimony of the Lord Jesus Himself in the Olivet discourse. In Matt. 24:15, He refers to "the abomination of desolation, spoken of through [*dia*] Daniel the prophet." The phrase "abomination of desolation" occurs three times in Daniel (9:27; 11:31; 12:11). If these words of Christ are reliably reported, we can only conclude that He believed the historic Daniel to be the personal author of the prophecies containing this phrase. No other interpretation is possible in the light of the preposition *dia*, which refers to personal agency. It is significant that Jesus regarded this "abomination" as something to be brought to pass in a future age rather than being simply the idol of Zeus set up by Antiochus in the temple, as the Maccabean theorists insist.[156]

While this has certainly been an overview of the evidence in favor of the authenticity of Daniel, there will never be enough to satisfy the critic. One professor at Oxford University wrote: "Nothing is gained by a mere answer to objections, so long as the original prejudice, 'there cannot be supernatural prophecy,' remains." What does this mean? It means that the critic is blinded by his prejudice. However, God has given them the choice of free will.

---

[155] Gleason Leonard Archer, *A Survey of Old Testament Introduction*, 3rd. ed.]. (Chicago: Moody Press, 1998), 445.

[156] Gleason Leonard Archer, *A Survey of Old Testament Introduction*, 3rd. ed.]. (Chicago: Moody Press, 1998), 444.

The Bible critics are ever so vigilant today. They are more prepared than most Christians and witness about their doubts far more than your average Christian witnesses about his or her faith.

**1 Peter 3:15** Updated American Standard Version (UASV)

15 but sanctify Christ as Lord in your hearts, always being prepared to make a defense[157] to anyone who asks you for a reason for the hope that is in you; yet do it with gentleness and respect;

Peter says that we must be prepared to make a *defense*. The Greek word behind the English "defense" is *apologia* (apologia), which is actually a legal term that refers to the defense of a defendant in court. Our English apologetics is just what Peter spoke of, having the ability to give a reason to any who may challenge us or to answer those who are not challenging us but who have honest questions that deserve to be answered.

To whom was the apostle Peter talking? Who was Peter saying needed always to be prepared to make a defense? Was he talking only to the pastors, elders, servants, or was he speaking to all Christians? Peter opens this letter saying, "to the chosen who are residing temporarily in the dispersion in Pontus, Galatia, Cappadocia, Asia, and Bithynia." Who are these "chosen" ones? The College Press NIV Commentary gives us the answer,

The Greek text does not include the word "God's," but the translation is a fair one since the clear implication is that God did the choosing. The word Peter uses has a rich biblical heritage. The Jews found their identity and the basis of their lives in the fact that they were God's chosen people (see, e.g., Deut 7:6–8). The New Testament frequently identifies Christians as elect or chosen. In 1 Peter 2:9 Peter will identify Christians as "a chosen people," using the same word ἐκλεκτός (*eklektos*) here translated "elect." The same word is also used of Christ in 2:4 and 6 (where it is translated "chosen"). Christians are chosen or elect through the chosen or elect One, Jesus Christ. The idea that Christians are God's chosen people is fundamental to Peter's thinking, as is apparent in 1:13–2:10. Peter is already laying the foundation for his appeals to these Christians to live up to their holy calling. (Black and Black 1998)

The "chosen who are residing temporarily in the dispersion" were Christians, who were living among **non-**Christian Jews and Gentiles. This letter, then, is addressed to all Christians, but the context of chapters 1:3 to 4:11 is mostly addressed to newly baptized Christians. Therefore, all Christians are obligated to 'be prepared to make a defense to anyone who

[157] Or *argument*; or *explanation*

asks us for a reason for the hope that is in us.' Yes, we are all required to defend our hope successfully.

# APPENDIX D Identifying the Antichrist

## What are the characteristics of the Antichrist?

If one were to ask different Christians what they believe about the Antichrist, different views would be on the subject. "Dispensationalists look for a future Roman ruler who will appear during the tribulation and will rule over the earth. Those in the Amillennialist School interpret the term symbolically."[158] It is more than these two choices, though, as some feel the Antichrist is one person while others feel that it is a group of people who are in opposition to Christ while others feel it is anyone that is "anti" Christ." Powerful people of the past have been labeled the Antichrist, such as the Roman Emperor Nero, Adolf Hitler, the German philosopher Friedrich Nietzsche, and radical Islam.[159] However, others are looking for a powerful world leader to come, or that is here but has not stepped out of the shadows, who will rule the world. For these ones, they point to Revelation chapter 13 as referring to the Antichrist,

## What About Revelation Chapter 13

**Revelation 13:18** Updated American Standard Version (UASV)

**18** Here is wisdom. Let the one who has understanding calculate the number of the beast, for it is the number of a man **[**the antichrist**]**, and his number is six hundred and sixty-six **[**666**]**.[160]

Let us start with the number 666. Notice first, we are not told the significance of the number six hundred and sixty-six. However, we are told here who will ascertain the importance of that number, the "one who has understanding." We do know some things. We know that "man" (Gk., *anthrōpos*), often signifies the whole of mankind, i.e., humanity. We also know that the number six in the Bible, one less than seven (perfect) can denote imperfection. We also know that when something is mentioned three times, it intensifies what is being said. Therefore, six hundred and sixty-six (666) could be signifying gross human imperfection. This would very much refer

---

158 http://biblia.com/books/hlmnillbbldict/Page.p_75

159 The Islamic Antichrist: The Shocking Truth about the Real Nature of the Beast by Richardson, Joel (Jul 28, 2009)

160 One early ms reads 616

to ones that are alienated from God, which would put some in opposition to Christ.

**Revelation Chapter 13**: In order for this chapter of Revelation alone to apply, the antichrist must just be one person, and we will soon discover that this just is not the case. Let us look at Revelation 13:2, "And the beast that I saw was like a leopard; its feet were like a bear's, and its mouth was like a lion's mouth. And to it the dragon gave his power and his throne and great authority." What do these features denote?

> The body parts of this brute are a composite of three of the four creatures of Daniel 7:1–6, but in reverse order: body of **a leopard**, feet of **a bear**, and mouth of **a lion. In** Daniel's vision, these represented historical empires that opposed Judah, such as Babylon and Persia. Here they are all combined into one monster—raw political-military power.
>
> The Christians of John's day immediately grasped that the form of the monster current in their day was Imperial Rome. Where did Rome's power come from? **The dragon gave the beast his power and his throne and great authority**. Although God has ordained that government is used for good (Rom. 13:1–7), clearly the devil has mastered the art of twisting what God means for good and turning it to evil.[161]

**Revelation 13:1** Updated American Standard Version (UASV)

1 And the dragon stood on the sand of the sea. Then I saw a beast coming up out of the sea, having ten horns and seven heads, and on his horns were ten diadems, and on his heads were blasphemous names.

What or who do these seven heads represent? The seven heads are seven world empires throughout Bible history that have had some impact on God's people, five of which were before John's day: Egypt, Assyria, Babylon, Medo-Persia, and Greece. The sixth of those world empires were in existence during John's day, Rome, with the seventh world empire yet to come. Look at John's reference again in the same book.

**Revelation 17:9-10** Updated American Standard Version (UASV)

9 Here is the mind which has wisdom. The seven heads are seven mountains on which the woman sits, **10** and they are seven kings; five have fallen [Egypt, Assyrian, Babylon, Medo-Persia, and Greece], one is [Rome],

[161] Kendell H. Easley, *Revelation, vol. 12, Holman New Testament Commentary* (Nashville, TN: Broadman & Holman Publishers, 1998), 227.

the other has not yet come [?]; and when he comes, he must remain a little while.

We can conclude that the first wild beast from the sea (vss. 1-10) and the second wild beast from the earth (vss. 11-18) of Revelation 13 represent two governmental powers. The first wild beast, "the dragon **[Satan, Rev. 12:3, 9]** gave it his power and his throne and great authority." The second wild beast "exercises all the authority of the first beast on his behalf and compels the earth and those who live on it to worship the first beast." Therefore, these beasts or governmental powers are against Christ. Consequently, they are antichrists.

## Antichrist Defined and Explained

We can now define the antichrist as anyone, any group, organization, or government that is *against* or *instead of* Christ or who mistreat his people. Thus, we are not just looking for one person, group, organization, or power.

The Bible does not refer to just one antichrist. There has been an innumerable number of antichrists since the apostle John wrote his letters at the end of the first century.

**1 John 2:18** Updated American Standard Version (UASV)

18 Little children, it is the last hour [John is the last of the 12 apostles and is almost a hundred, close to death]; and just as you heard that antichrist is coming, even now many antichrists have arisen; whereby we know that it is the last hour [of John's protection (the apostolic period), as he dies shortly thereafter].

As is spelled out within the text, "the last hour," John was referring to the apostolic period of the twelve apostles. At the time of this writing, about 98 C.E., all of the other apostles are dead, and John is close to one hundred years old. The apostolic period was a time when the twelve apostles could protect the Christian congregation from the upcoming great apostasy that Jesus and the New Testament writers warned was coming. New Testament textual scholar Philip Comfort comments on this,

> Once the final, authorized publication was released and distributed to the churches, I think it unlikely that any substantive changes would have occurred during the lifetime of the apostles or second-generation coworkers. By "substantive," I mean a change that would alter Christian doctrine or falsify an apostolic account. The primary reason is that the writers (or their immediate successors) were alive at the time and therefore could challenge any

significant, unauthorized alterations. As long as eyewitnesses such as John or Peter were alive, who would dare change any of the Gospel accounts in any significant manner? Anyone among the Twelve could have testified against any falsification. And there was also a group of 72 other disciples (Luke 10:1) who could do the same. Furthermore, according to 1 Corinthians 15:6, Jesus had at least five hundred followers by the time he had finished his ministry, and these people witnessed Jesus in resurrection. Most of these people were still alive (Paul said) in AD 57/58 (the date of composition for 1 Corinthians); it stands to reason that several lived for the next few decades—until the turn of the century and even beyond.[162]

**2 John 1:7** Updated American Standard Version (UASV)

7 For many deceivers have gone out into the world, even those who do not confess the coming of Jesus Christ in the flesh. This is the deceiver and the antichrist.

We also notice that John says there are "many antichrists." John refers to these collectively as "the antichrist" here in 2 John 1:7. Should Christians be looking for some future time, to identify some specific antichrist?

**1 John 4:3** Updated American Standard Version (UASV)

3 and every spirit that does not confess Jesus is not from God; this is the spirit of the antichrist, of which you have heard that it is coming, and now it is in the world already.

First John was written in the last years of the first century, about 98 C.E., and yet John says that there were antichrists already in the world during his day. It is the signs of antichrists in John's day, which let him know it was the last hour. What characteristics do the antichrists have?

**1 John 2:22** Updated American Standard Version (UASV)

22 Who is the liar but the one who denies that Jesus is the Christ? This is the antichrist, even the one who denies the Father and the Son.

Clearly, any who deny that Jesus is the Messiah or Christ, the anointed one, the unique Son of God is the antichrist.

**1 John 2:18-19** Updated American Standard Version (UASV)

18 Little children, it is the last hour; and just as you heard that antichrist is coming, even now many antichrists have arisen; whereby we know that it

---

162 Philip Comfort, *Encountering the Manuscripts: An Introduction to New Testament Paleography & Textual Criticism* (Nashville, TN: Broadman & Holman, 2005), 255–256.

is the last hour. [19] They went out from us, but they were not of us; for if they had been of us, they would have continued with us; but they went out, so that they would be revealed that they all are not of us.

Apostates are any who stand off from the truth, who also go a step further by attacking their former brothers of the faith. In the above, we see John is talking about apostates being among the antichrists, as he specifically said in verse 18 that 'even now there are many antichrists,' followed by verse 19 that says, "they went out from us." Those who went out from them were ones, who had abandoned the first-century Christian congregation. This would then also include "the man of lawlessness" also known as the "the lawless one," or "son of destruction" described by Paul. (2 Thess. 2:3, 8) In addition, it would also include "false teachers among you, who will secretly bring in destructive heresies, even denying the Master who bought them." (2 Pet. 2:1) See Identifying the Man of Lawlessness in Chapter 5.

**John 15:20-21** Updated American Standard Version (UASV)

[20] Remember the word that I said to you: 'A servant is not greater than his master.' If they **persecuted me**, they **will also persecute you**. If they kept my word, they will keep yours also. [21] But all these things they will do to you on account of my name, because they do not know the one who sent me.

**Psalm 2:2** Updated American Standard Version (UASV)

[2] The kings of the earth take their stand,
and the rulers take counsel together,
against Jehovah and against his anointed one [Messiah or Christ] , saying,

**Matthew 24:23-26** Updated American Standard Version (UASV)

[23] Then if any man says to you, 'Look, here is the Christ!' or 'There he is!' do not believe it. [24] For **false Christs** and false prophets will arise and will show great signs and wonders, so as to mislead, if possible, even the chosen ones.[163] [25] Behold, I have told you in advance. [26] So if they say to you, 'Behold, he is in the wilderness,' do not go out, or, 'Behold, he is in the inner rooms,' do not believe it.

Jesus' prophecy about the end of the Jewish age **of his day** and the end of wicked humanity **in our day**, reads, "See that no one leads you astray. For many will come in my name, saying, 'I am the Christ,' and they will **lead many astray**." (Matt 24:4-5) Here in our current verses, Jesus tells us who specifically is being "led astray," "For false Christs [Gr., *pseudochristoi*] and

[163] Or *the elect*

false prophets will arise and will show great signs and wonders, so as to mislead, if possible, even **the chosen ones**." Any who falsely claim to be Christ (anointed one or Messiah), or claim to be a special representative of Christ, are included in the "antichrist" [Gr., *antichristos*], which as we have already seen is mentioned five times by the apostle John. – 1 John 2:18, 22; 4:3; 2 John 1:7.

There were false Christs and false prophets that came on the scene before 70 C.E. and the destruction of the Jewish age. Jewish historian Flavius Josephus confirms this as he writes that before the Romans ever attacked, false Messiahs prompted rebellion. To mention just a couple, there is Menahem ben Judah, who claimed to be the Jewish Messiah and is mentioned by Josephus. Then, there is Theudas, who claimed to be the Messiah, a Jewish rebel of the 1st century C.E., who, between 44 and 46 CE, led his followers in a short-lived revolt. However, as is self-evident, they showed themselves to be false, charlatans, as they did not deliver the Jewish people from the Roman armies. After the destruction of Jerusalem, up unto this day, the Jews[164] have not put faith in Jesus Christ, the Son of God, but have rather continued their search for a Messiah in the flesh.

Conversely, both Jewish and non-Jewish Christians have evidenced their faith in Jesus Christ, as they have continued to look at the end of Satan's rule over the earth, the end of wicked humankind, the return of Jesus Christ and his millennial reign. There have been many notable people in the 18th to the 21st century, who has been claimed to be the reincarnation or incarnation of Jesus or the Second Coming of Christ. Either they have made these claims, or their followers have made a claim. To mention just a couple, Jim Jones (1931–1978), founder of Peoples Temple, this started as a branch of a mainstream Protestant group before becoming a cult. Then, we have Marshall Applewhite (1931–1997), an American, who posted a famous message declaring, "I, Jesus, Son of God," whose Heaven's Gate cult committed mass suicide on March 26, 1997. Wayne Bent (1941–), AKA Michael Travesser of the Lord Our Righteousness Church. He claimed, "I am the embodiment of God. I am divinity and humanity combined."

If any reader does not believe that they can fall victim to charismatic persons, they are deceiving themselves. Millions of Christians have fallen victim to such ones, and they have not even had the satanic power of 'showing great signs and wonders,' which will be the result before humanity's "great tribulation." Then, we have Christians that pick up these end-times books, going around speaking of how much truth are within them when the

[164] This is not to say that no individual Jewish persons have not converted to Christianity, as hundreds of thousands have in the last two millennium.

author(s) has gone beyond what the Word of God says. Finally, Pentecostals and Charismatic Christians number over 500 million, a quarter of the world's two billion Christians. This author sees the religious leaders of these groups as the false Christs, antichrists, false prophets that will be the catalyst to the major false Christs, antichrists, false prophets before the great tribulation. **Excessive** emotionalism within Christianity brings about a blind desire for the return of Christ, opening many up to a situation in which religious leaders offer biblical passages that incorrectly match a return of Christ, e.g. signs of the times, a charismatic person, world events, bad prooftexting, and the like.

Thus, the antichrist is any person, group, organization, or power.

(1) The antichrist denies that Jesus is the Christ,

(2) The antichrist denies the Father and the Son,

(3) Some of the antichrists have abandoned the Christian faith, and after that work in opposition to Christ,

(4) The antichrist is anti-Christian

## How Can We Identify the Antichrist?

**1 John 2:18** Updated American Standard Version (UASV)

[18] Little children, it is the last hour; and just as you heard that **antichrist is coming**, even now **many antichrists** have arisen; whereby we know that it is the last hour.

If we were sitting by the radio, and the newscaster came on to warn us about an escaped murderer from the county jail, we would listen intently as they described what he looked like. We would be very cautious until we heard he had been captured.

As Christians, we have received a very similar warning about the Antichrist being on the loose, and we want to listen intently as the Bible tells us about how we can identify him, her, or it. John writes, "Every spirit that does not confess Jesus is not from God; this is the spirit of the antichrist, of which you have heard that it is coming, and now it is in the world already." (UASV) Was the Antichrist in the world only in the tomb of the apostle John, or is the Antichrist present now, or is the Antichrist coming at a future time?

John alone who uses the term "Antichrist," which he does five times. From those five times, we gather this entity is "against" (i.e., denies Christ) or "instead of" (i.e., false Christs) Jesus Christ. The Bible gives us clear insight into the Antichrist, but interpreters have run amuck into speculation as we saw in the introduction.

## Misidentifying the Antichrist

The greatest misidentification has been the interpretation that the Antichrist is just one particular person. Moreover, there have been many who have been suggested as contenders. Early on, it was thought that Roman Emperor Nero was the Antichrist. He was definitely antichristian, which is, in essence, an antichrist. Jesus said, "If they persecuted me, they will also persecute you." (John 15:20) More recently, it was suggested that Adolf Hitler was the Antichrist. Again, Hitler was certainly antichristian. Many have pointed to Revelation 13 in reference to the Antichrist, but they are not so in the sense that many might think. Yes, these beasts or governmental powers of Revelation 13 are against Christ.

Consequently, they are antichrists, as we saw in chapter 1. However, some suggest that the mark of the beat, 666, will be the mark of the Antichrist. Yes, while chapter 1 helped us appreciate what 666 might stand for, it does not fit the misidentification of the Antichrist being but one person. It does fit the biblical truth that there are many antichrists, i.e., many humans in opposition to Christ, by way of their gross human imperfection.

## Who Make Up the Antichrist?

When Jesus came to the earth, he had to face many enemies; Herod, who tried to have Jesus killed as a child, Satan, who followed him into the wilderness to tempt him, the Jewish religious leaders, and eventually the Roman government by way of Pontius Pilate. Even though Jesus returned to heaven, and is now untouchable, he still has many enemies. The apostle John stated,

**1 John 2:22** Updated American Standard Version (ASV)

22 Who is the liar but the one who denies that Jesus is the Christ? This is the antichrist, even the one who denies the Father and the Son.

The Bible speaks of apostasy, which is one who stands off from what is true. Thus, we would refer to one of these as an apostate. Michael Fink writes, "In 2 Thess. 2:3 Paul addressed those who had been deceived into believing that the day of the Lord had already come. He taught that apostasy would precede the day of the Lord. The Spirit had explicitly revealed this falling away from the faith (1 Tim. 4:1). Such apostasy in the latter times will involve doctrinal deception, moral insensitivity, and ethical departures from God's truth." (Brand, Draper and Archie 2003, 87) These are ones that come in many shades of doctrinal deceit. They reject clear teachings of Scripture and spread false teachings about the Father and the Son. Therefore, they are a part of the antichrist. Jesus forewarned his disciples, and by implication us,

**Luke 21:12** Updated American Standard Version (UASV)

12 But before **all these things**, they will lay their hands on you and will persecute you, delivering you to the synagogues and prisons, bringing you before kings and governors for My name's sake.

"All these things" is referring to the events of 21:7-11, which is a reference to the destruction of Jerusalem in 70 C.E.[165] Thus, "Before international warfare and natural chaos come, the church will face persecution, Jesus continued. Belief in Christ and his name will be cause enough for you to be put in jail and punished by the government. Jewish religious leaders will join forces with the government to make this happen." (Buter 2000, 351) This happened to the first century Christians, but by implication, if the world hated them because of bearing the name of Christ, how much more so would this not be the case in end times. Are Christians not suffering persecution in this liberal-progressive world that is not emerging? Yes, listen to the principle as Paul laid it out,

**2 Timothy 3:12** Updated American Standard Version (UASV)

12 Indeed, all who desire to live a godly life in Christ Jesus will be persecuted,

Those that are of gross human imperfection, 666, because they are alienated from God by heart and mind, cause such mistreatment. In other words, they are working "against" Christ, making them a part of the antichrist. Jesus himself said, "He who is not with me is against me." Those who are antichrists have one outcome in the end.

## The Destruction of Antichrist

**Psalm 5:6** Updated American Standard Version (UASV)

6 You destroy those who speak lies;
Jehovah abhors the bloodthirsty and deceitful man.

The apostle John wrote,

165 See Acts 5:36; 21:38

**2 John 1:7** Updated American Standard Version (UASV)

7 For many deceivers have gone out into the world, even those who do not confess the coming of Jesus Christ in the flesh. This is the deceiver and the antichrist.

Those who are lying and deceiving, the antichrists, the Father by way of the Son will bring destruction upon them. As we move through these last days, true Christians should be well prepared not to allow anti-Christian trickery treachery, and pressure to cause them to have a spiritual shipwreck. The apostle John warns us,

**2 John 1:8-9** Updated American Standard Version (UASV)

8 Watch yourselves, that you do not lose what we have worked for, but that you may receive a full reward. 9 Everyone who goes on ahead and does not remain in the teaching of Christ, does not have God; the one who remains in the teaching, he has both the Father and the Son.

There is always the danger of being turned aside from the truth to apostasy. On this, David Walls and Max Anders write, "To heed the teachings of these antichrists results not in the loss of salvation but in the loss of spiritual reward. God would not forget what they had done for him: "God is not unjust; he will not forget your work and the love you have shown him as you have helped his people" (Heb. 6:10). Yet, to depart from the rewardable path is to lose the full reward coming to those who do not follow such false teachers (1 Cor. 3:8, 11–15). The antichrists—the false teachers and false prophets talked about more thoroughly in 1 John—were running ahead, and were not continuing **in the teaching of Christ. Runs ahead** is also translated "goes too far" (nasb) or "transgresses" (NKJV). These give a more complete understanding of the danger. The teaching of Christ may refer to the teachings of Jesus or to teachings about Jesus. In either case, it refers to orthodox truth established and accepted in the church. The text seems to center on defection from the truth by those who had once held to the truth. Some teachers believe this refers to Christians who depart from the faith. If this is the case, to deviate from the truth would be to leave God behind. In the sense of fellowship and blessing, the person who defects from the faith **does not have God.** This position does not suggest loss of salvation but points to doctrinal deviation and disobedience. Other Bible teachers believe the one who **runs ahead** is not a true Christian. He may have given every appearance of being a true Christian, but his defection from the faith proves he never was a true believer. This seems more in keeping with the teaching of 1 John. Scripture seeks those who learn and practice the true teachings, those who fully understand who Jesus is. Jesus is equal with God the Father.

To have Jesus is to have the Father, and to have the Father is to have Jesus (see commentary on 1 John 5:20)."[166]

## The Antichrist is Further Identified

Christians not only have to battle the Agnostic and atheist, but they must also contend with liberal Bible scholars, and even some moderates, who use higher criticism in their interpretation. It is here that we should also expound a little more on the "criticism" portion of the term "higher criticism" and "textual criticism." It might be more helpful if we talk for a moment about biblical criticism. It is divided into two branches: lower criticism and higher criticism. Lower criticism, also known as textual criticism, is an investigation of manuscripts by those known as textual scholars, seeking to establish the original reading, which is no longer available. Higher criticism, also known as literary criticism, takes that original text that has been established by textual criticism, looking for any sources that may lie behind it.

**Lower criticism** (i.e., textual criticism), has been the bedrock of scholarship over the last 500 years, which has given us a master text, i.e., a critical text, which is a 99.95 percent reflection of the original published Greek New Testament. It has contributed to the furtherance of Bible scholarship, removing interpolations, correcting scribal errors, and giving us a critical text, allowing us to produce better translations of the New and Old Testaments.

In contrast, **higher criticism** (i.e., literary criticism) has unlocked the floodgates of pseudo-scholarly works whose consequence has been to weaken, challenge and undercut Christian's confidence in the Scriptures. In an effort to determine the origin of each book, its author, its location where it was written, and how much can be attributed to the traditional author, the sources behind a Bible book, higher criticism has destroyed the trustworthiness of the Bible, picking it apart until there is little left. Fortunately, some conservative scholars[167] have **undermined** these higher critics for their illogical, unreasonable lack of common sense that they have had as they have attempted their dissecting of God's Word. Many of higher criticism does not believe in literal antichrists, but rather sees it as merely a

---

[166] David Walls and Max Anders, *I & II Peter, I, II & III John, Jude*, vol. 11, Holman New Testament Commentary (Nashville, TN: Broadman & Holman Publishers, 1999), 237–238.

[167] Such scholars as Robert L. Thomas, Norman L. Geisler, Gleason L. Archer, F. David Farnell, and Joseph M. Holden, et al. have fought for decades, to educate us about the dangers of higher criticism.

concept of good versus evil, and to these critics, the idea of a literal antichrist is nothing more than a myth.

**Matthew 24:23-26** Updated American Standard Version (UASV)

[23] Then if anyone says to you, 'Look, here is the Christ!' or 'There he is!' do not believe it. [24] For false Christs and false prophets will arise and will show great signs and wonders, so as to mislead, if possible, even the chosen ones. [25] Behold, I have told you beforehand. [26] So if they say to you, 'Behold, He is in the wilderness,' do not go out, or, 'Behold, He is in the inner rooms,' do not believe it.

So that false Christs and false prophets may not fool the chosen ones of God or those who are truly Christian, Jesus gave us the warning found here in Matthew. Those who are claiming that they are Christ himself, the return of Christ, are the false Christs. On the other hand, false prophets are those that claim that God reveals the truth to them and them alone.

It is right before and during the Great Tribulation when we will hear reports that Christ has returned. There will be both false Christs and prophets, who will be used by Satan to carry out great signs and miracles, a so-called evident demonstration of their real credentials as the Christ or a prophet of Christ. These false ones will present such a showy display that even true Christians will fall for their deception. We need to understand because one may have the ability to perform miracles; this does not mean the miracles are from God. – Matthew 7:21-23

We have seen that Christians are easily swayed into mere charismatic personalities. How much more so would they be deceived by a charismatic person, who can also perform miracles and signs. Millions of Christians flock to mega-churches and televangelists, such as Joel Osteen, Benny Hinn, Paul and Jan Crouch, Pat Robinson, Jimmy Swaggart, Ted Haggard, Jim and Tammy Baker, and Joyce Meyer. Moreover, tens of millions will be the first to buy a book about end times, the last days, the prophecy of the Great Tribulation and Armageddon, such as *The Harbinger: The Ancient Mystery That Holds the Secret of America's Future.* These Christians will come to church with books likes these under their arms, swearing up and down that every word is so true, convincing others to buy into the lie.

Write a book about the last days, and it becomes a New York Times Bestselling book. Be a Bible scholar who puts ten years of research into a book on the historical reliability of Jesus' resurrection, and he will sell a few thousand books. These writers of the end times, last days, Great Tribulation and Armageddon are a foretaste of what is to come. In their books, these authors come across as though they have been given information directly from God, a special insight, which allows them to disclose these so-called mysterious secrets. If tens of millions of Christians drink down these books and the televangelist, as if they are quenching their thirst, there is little doubt that Jesus' warning will do them any good.

**2 Thessalonians 2:3, 7, 9** Updated American Standard Version (UASV)

3 Let no one deceive[168] you in any way, for it will not come unless the
apostasy[169] comes first, and the man of lawlessness is revealed, the son of
destruction, 7 For the mystery[170] of lawlessness is already at work; but only
until the one who is right now acting as a restraint is out of the way. 9 namely,
the one whose coming[171] is in accordance with the activity of Satan, with all
power and signs and false wonders,

**Antichrist Equals Anti ("Instead of or "against") Christ**

**Matthew 16:16** Updated American Standard Version (UASV)

16 Simon Peter answered, "You are the Christ, the Son of the living God."

The Christ [Heb. Messiah anointed one] that Peter spoke of and was/is being opposed; he is the one spoken of by the prophets. He was born in Bethlehem around 1 B.C.E., began his ministry in 29 C.E., gave his life as a ransom for many in 33 C.E., and was resurrected on the third day, and ascended back to heaven 40 days after his resurrection.

Looking a little deeper into the term, "antichrist," it seems that it has two meanings. It does have the meaning of "anti," "against," "opposed to," but the preposition also carries the meaning "instead of." Thus, we are looking for ones or groups that are "against" Jesus Christ or his disciples. However, we are also looking for ones who are "instead of" Christ, a false or pseudo-Christ. As we have seen from the two previous chapters, many believe that the antichrist is one individual person who is still yet to come.

---

168 Or *seduce*

169 **Apostasy**: (Gr. *apostasia*) The term literally means "to stand away from" and is used to refer to ones who 'stand away from the truth.' It is abandonment, a rebellion, an apostasy, a refusal to accept or acknowledge true worship. In Scripture, this is used primarily concerning the one who rises up in defiance of the only true God and his people, working in opposition to the truth.–Ac 21:21; 2 Thess. 2:3.

170 **Mystery; Secret**: (Gr. *mystērion*) A sacred divine mystery or secret doctrine that lies with God alone, which is withheld from both the angelic body and humans, until the time he determines that it is to be revealed, and to those to whom he chooses to make it known.–Mark 4:11; Rom. 11:25; 16:25; 1 Cor. 2:1; 4:1; 13:2; 14:2; 15:51; Eph. 1:9; 6:19; Col. 1:26; 2:2; 2 Thess. 2:7; 1 Tim. 3:9; Rev. 17:5.

171 See note on 2:8.

However, we have also seen that antichrist applies to all persons who claim to be the one and only representative or Christ or coming in place of Christ, as well as all persons, groups or organizations that are *opposed* to Christ. Again, Jesus said, "He who is not with me is against me" (Matt 12:30) In this verse, Stuart K. Weber writes, "Jesus eliminated the possibility of anyone remaining "neutral" toward him. Anyone who was not seeking to live for Jesus was, by default, Jesus enemy." (Weber 2000, 177)

**Hebrews 5:13-14** Updated American Standard Version (UASV)

13 For everyone who partakes of milk is unacquainted with the word of righteousness, for he is an infant. **14** But solid food belongs to the mature, to those who through practice have their discernment trained to distinguish between good and evil.

The milk metaphor is easy for every generation because we all know that a babe grows into physical maturity by the milk that he consumes. So too, the spiritual babe grows into maturity by taking in the metaphorical milk of elementary Bible doctrine. Once they have reached maturity, they can then take in "solid food," deeper Bible truths. Paul tells us at 1 Corinthians 13:11, "When I was a child, I spoke like a child, I thought like a child, I reasoned like a child. When I became a man, I gave up childish ways." These Hebrew Christians needed to get off the elementary Bible doctrines ("milk") and move on to the deeper biblical truths of "solid food."

If we are to appreciate and apply the Bible in our lives, we must first fully understand it. We must know what the author of a Bible book meant by the words that he used, as it should have been understood by his original intended audience. Then, we will be able to attach the significance that it has for our lives. Suppose we are unaware of the correct way of interpreting the Scriptures, grammatical-historical interpretation. In that case, we are going to be one of those who Peter spoke of as, 'the ignorant and unstable, who twist the Scriptures to their own destruction.' Tens of millions of Christians unknowingly share an incorrect understanding of Scripture every day, because they are not aware of the rules and principles of interpretation, while others may be aware of some yet fail to apply them correctly.

## The Antichrist and Religions

The Scriptures are very clear as to who Jesus was/is, and those who claim that he was merely a human in history, rejecting his divinity, are antichrists. All, who willfully manipulate Scriptures to get it to say what they want it to say, are guilty of theological bias, and is the antichrist. Devotees of Oriental religions, atheists, deists[172] or agnostics, are antichrists.

| **John 1:14** (UASV) | **Galatians 4:4** (UASV) |
|---|---|
| 14 And the Word became flesh and dwelt among us, and we have seen his glory, glory as of the only begotten one from the Father, full of grace and truth. | 4 But when the fullness of time came, God sent forth his Son, born of a woman, born under the law, |

Anyone who denies the value of Jesus' ransom sacrifice is an antichrist. John the Baptist said of Jesus, "Behold, the Lamb of God, who takes away the sin of the world!" (John 1:29) Jesus said of himself, "the Son of Man came … to give his life as a ransom for many." (Matt 20:28) The apostle John wrote, "The blood of Jesus his Son cleanses us from all sin." (1 John 1:7) The apostle Peter said of Jesus, "but with the precious blood of Christ, like that of a lamb without blemish or spot." (1 Pet. 1:19) The apostle Paul wrote, "God shows his love for us in that while we were still sinners, Christ died for us. Since, therefore, we have now been justified by his blood, much more shall we be saved by him from the wrath of God." (Rom. 5:8-9) Isaiah, prophesied,

**Isaiah 53:12** Updated American Standard Version (UASV)

12 Therefore I will divide him a portion with the many,
and he shall divide the spoil with the strong,
because he poured out his soul to death
and was numbered with the transgressors;
yet he bore the sin of many,
and makes intercession for the transgressors.

Whether we wish to accept it or not, a number of religious leaders, from a number of Christian denominations reject the atoning work of Christ. Some even believe the teaching of the atonement is offensive to their moral senses. They say that the death of Jesus Christ was not needed for human salvation.

They even say that Scripture does not teach that Christians receive a righteous standing with God because of Jesus' death. These ones would be antichrists, as atonement is a biblical "doctrine that God has reconciled sinners to Himself through the sacrificial work of Jesus Christ." (Brand, Draper and Archie 2003, 142)

---

172 Deism is a belief in God based on reason rather than revelation and involving the view, which God has set the universe in motion but does not interfere with how it runs.

**Acts 20:28-30** Revised Standard Version (RSV)

[28] Take heed to yourselves and to all the flock, in which the Holy Spirit has made you overseers, to care for the church of God which he obtained with the blood of his own Son. [29] I know that after my departure fierce wolves will come in among you, not sparing the flock; [30] and **from among your own selves** will arise men **speaking perverse things**, to **draw away the disciples after them**.

Yes, Jesus was warning of the coming danger, of ones who were out to steal those who are his disciples. They too are his enemy, trying to take his disciples for them. Jesus repeats his warning twice, "by their fruit you will recognize them." (Matt. 7:16, 20) The distinguishing marker is good versus bad (literally worthless, rotten) fruit.

The main good fruit is mentioned in verse 21, only those, who are doing the will of the Father, are producing good fruit. Another fruit is the God's Word itself. As Jesus said, so it is, "If you continue in my word you are truly my disciples, and you will know the truth, and the truth will set you free." (John 8:31-32) Yes, genuine Christians "must worship in spirit and truth." – John 4:24

How do we "worship in spirit and truth"? We worship in spirit when a heart filled with faith and love motivates our life course, our walking with God. This means that we are completely devoted to pure worship as it is revealed in Scripture. In addition, to worship in spirit means that we allow our lives to be guided by the Spirit-inspired Word of God. Through Bible study, prayer, and worship, as well as the application of God's Word, our spirit, the new person, must be in harmony with God's Spirit. We worship in truth by coming to an accurate knowledge of the Word of God and following its revealed truths, not man. We need to reject the false teachings that have infiltrated into the Way (Ac 9:2; 19:9) and the Truth (3 John 1:4). If this means that we discover our form of Christianity is not in harmony with the spirit and truth of God, we must choose another course. This means that if we have had a mistaken view of the antichrist all along, we must now humbly accept the truth as Scripture has clearly stated.

Yes, those, who standoff from the Truth and the Way, would not be seeking their own disciples, but rather they would be seeking "to draw away the disciples after them." i.e., the disciples of Christ. Jesus was well aware that the easiest way to defeat any group is to divide them, and so was Satan, who had been watching humanity for over 4,000 years, and especially the Israelites (Isaac and Ishmael / Jacob and Esau / Israel and Judah), as "Satan disguises himself as an angel of light. So it is no surprise if his servants, also, disguise themselves as servants of righteousness."—2 Corinthians 11:14-15

The apostle Peter also spoke of these things about **64 C.E.**, "there will be false teachers among you, who will secretly bring in destructive heresies . . . in their greed they will exploit you with false words.." (2 Pet. 2:1, 3) These abandoned the faithful words, became false teachers, rising within the Christian congregation, sharing their corrupting influence, intending to hide, disguise, or mislead.

These dire warnings by Jesus and the New Testament authors had their beginnings in the first century C.E. Yes, the false teachers, causing division, began small, but burst forth on the scene in the second century. Paul wrote,

**2 Thessalonians 2:3-4** Updated American Standard Version (UASV)

3 Let no one deceive[173] you in any way, for it will not come unless the apostasy[174] comes first, and the man of lawlessness is revealed, the son of destruction, 4 who opposes and exalts himself against every so-called god or object of worship, so that he takes his seat in the temple of God, showing himself as being God.

**"[Paul says it] Is Already at Work"**

About **51 C.E.**, some 18-years after Jesus' death, resurrection and ascension, division was already starting to creep into the faith, "the mystery of lawlessness is already at work." (2 Thess. 2:7) Yes, the power of **the man of lawlessness** was already present, which is the power of Satan, the god of this world (2 Cor. 4:3-4), and his tens of millions of demons, are hard at work behind the scenes.

There were even some divisions beginning as early as **49 C.E.**, when the elders wrote a letter to the Gentile believers, saying,

> Since we have heard that some persons have gone out from us and troubled you with words, unsettling your minds, although we gave them no instructions (Ac 15:24)

Here we see that some *within* were being very vocal about their opposition to the direction the faith was heading. Here, it was over whether

[173] Or *seduce*

[174] **Apostasy**: (Gr. *apostasia*) The term literally means "to stand away from" and is used to refer to ones who 'stand away from the truth.' It is abandonment, a rebellion, an apostasy, a refusal to accept or acknowledge true worship. In Scripture, this is used primarily concerning the one who rises up in defiance of the only true God and his people, working in opposition to the truth.–Ac 21:21; 2 Thess. 2:3.

the Gentiles needed to be circumcised, suggesting that they needed to be obedient to the Mosaic Law.—Acts 15:1, 5

As the years progressed throughout the first-century, this divisive "talk [would] spread like gangrene." (2 Tim. 2:17, **c. 65 C.E.**) About **51 C.E.**, They had some in Thessalonica, at worst, going ahead of, or at best, misunderstanding Paul, and wrongly stating by word and a bogus letter "that the day of the Lord has come." (2 Thess. 2:1-2) In Corinth, about **55 C.E.**, "some of [were saying] that there is no resurrection of the dead. (1 Cor. 15:12) About **65 C.E.**, some were "saying that the resurrection has already happened. They [were] upsetting the faith of some." (2 Tim 2:16-18)

Throughout the next three decades, no inspired books were written. However, by the time the apostle John writes his three letters in 96-98 C.E., he tells us "Now many antichrists have come. Therefore we know that it is the last hour." (1 John 2:18) Again, these are ones "who denies that Jesus is the Christ" and ones who not confess "Jesus Christ has come in the flesh is from God." (1 John 2:22; 4:2-3)

From 33 C.E. to 100 C.E., the apostles served Christ as a restraint against "the apostasy" that was coming. Paul stated at 2 Thessalonians 2:7, "For the mystery of lawlessness is already at work. Only he [Apostle by Christ] who now restrains it [the apostasy] will do so until he **[apostles]** is out of the way." 2 Thessalonians 2:3 said, "Let no one deceive you in any way **[misinterpretation or false teachers of Paul's first letter]**. For that day **[presence, parousia (second coming) of Christ]** will not come, unless the apostasy comes first, and the man of lawlessness **[likely one person, or maybe an organization/movement, empowered by Satan]** is revealed, the son of destruction."

Again, we must keep in mind that the meaning of any given text is what the author meant by the words that he used, as should have been understood by his audience, and had some relevance/meaning for his audience. The rebellion [apostasy] began slowly in the first century and would break forth after the last apostle's death, i.e., John. Christianity would become one again, a universal religion, i.e., Catholicism. As a historian, Ariel Durant informed us earlier, by 187 C.E., there were 20 varieties of Christianity, and by 384 C.E., there were 80 varieties of Christianity. Today, we have over 41,000 varieties of Christianity.

## Outline of Christian Divisions

Start of Apostasy - 2nd Century

**Roman Catholic Church**

- 4th Century (Constantine)
- 5th Century Coptic
  - Jacobite
- 1054 C.E. Eastern Orthodox
  - Russian
  - Greek
  - Romanian and others
- 16th Century Reformation
  - Lutheran
  - German
  - Swedish
  - American and others
  - Anglican
  - Episcopal
  - Methodist
  - Salvation Army
  - Baptist
  - Pentecostal
  - Congregational
  - Calvinism
  - Presbyterian
  - Reformed Churches

## Pre-Reformation

- **Bishop Agobard** of Lyons, France (779-840), was against image worship, churches dedicated to saints and church liturgy that was contrary to Scripture.

- **Bishop Claudius** (d. between 827 and 839 C.E.)

- **Archdeacon Bérenger**, or Berengarius, of Tours, France (11th century C.E.), excommunicated as a heretic in 1050

- **Peter of Bruys** (1117-c. 1131), left the church because he disagreed with infant baptism, transubstantiation, prayers for the dead, worship of the cross and the need for church buildings.

- **Henry of Lausanne** (died imprisoned around 1148), spoke out against church liturgy, the corrupt clergy and the religious hierarchy.

- **Peter Waldo** (c. 1140–c. 1218) and the Waldenses, rejected purgatory, Masses for the dead, papal pardons and indulgences, and the worship of Mary and the saints.

- **John Wycliffe** (c. 1330-1384) preached against corruption in the monastic orders, papal taxation, the doctrine of transubstantiation (the doctrine that the bread and wine of Communion become, in substance, but not appearance, the body and blood of Jesus Christ at consecration), the confession, and church involvement in temporal affairs.

- **Jan Hus** (c. 1369-1415) preached against the corruption of the Roman Church and stressed the importance of reading the Bible. This swiftly fetched the anger of the hierarchy upon him. In 1403, the church leaders ordered him to stop preaching the antipapal notions of Wycliffe, whose books they had openly burned. Hus, nevertheless, went on to pen some of the most hurtful impeachments against the Church and their practices, such as the sale of indulgences. He was condemned and excommunicated in 1410.

## Reformation

- **Girolamo Savonarola** (1452-98) was of the San Marcos Monastery in Florence, Italy, spoke out against the corruption in the Church.

- **Martin Luther** (1483-1546) was a monk-scholar, was also a doctor of theology and a professor of Biblical studies at the University of

Wittenberg. He took issue with papal indulgences, power, purgatory, plenary remission of all penalties of the pope, among many other issues.

- **Ulrich Zwingli** (1484-1531) was a Catholic priest, who agreed with Luther in many doctrinal areas, in addition to the removal of all vestiges of the Roman Church: images, crucifixes, clerical garb, and even liturgical music. However, he disagreed with Luther's literal interpretation of the Eucharist, or Mass (Communion), as he said it "must be taken figuratively or metaphorically; 'This is my body,' means, 'The bread signifies my body,' or 'is a figure of my body.'" This one issue caused them to part ways.

- **Anabaptists** (i.e., rejected infant baptism, so rebaptized adults, *ana* meaning "again" in Greek), **Mennonites** (Dutch Reformer Menno Simons), and **Hutterites** (Tyrolean Jacob Hutter), felt that the Reformers did not go far enough in rejecting the failings of the Catholic Church.

- **John Calvin** (1509-64) published *Institutes of the Christian Religion*, in which he summarized the ideas of the early church fathers and medieval theologians, as well as those of Luther and Zwingli. His theological views would take too much space. John Calvin had Michael Servetus burned to death as a heretic. Calvin defended his actions in these words: "When the papists are so harsh and violent in defense of their superstitions that they rage cruelly to shed innocent blood, are not Christian magistrates shamed to show themselves less ardent in defense of the sure truth?" Calvin's religious extremism and personal hatred made him unwilling to see and understand the radicalness of his judgments and choked out and Christian principles.

- **William Tyndale** (1494-1536) had to flee from England, published his New Testament in 1526, and completed most of the Old Testament after his betrayal and arrest, in a dungeon. He would be strangled at the stake, and his body was burned. The 1611 King James Version was actually 97 percent Tyndale's translation. He denounced the practice of prayer to saints. He taught justification by faith, the return of Christ, and mortality of the soul.

- **Jacobus Arminius** (1560-1609), graduated from Holland's Leiden University, after which he spent six years in Switzerland, studying theology under Théodore de Bèze, the successor to Protestant Reformer John Calvin. Rather than support Calvinism, he went against it, especially the doctrine of predestination, which was at the core of Calvinism.

## Catholicism Summary

Roman Catholicism has tainted itself with its history of immorality and bloodshed and its pagan-tainted religious ideas and practices. The centuries-long oppression, torture, rape, pillage, and murder of tens of millions of men, women, and children cannot come from true Christianity. They were the biggest offenders of the apostasy that Paul said had to come before the return of Christ.

## Protestantism Summary

The Reformation gave us a return to the Bible in the common person's languages, which the Catholic Church had locked up in the dead language of Latin for 500-years. The Reformers brought the common folk freedom from papal authority but also from many erroneous Bible doctrines and dogmas that had gone on for a thousand years. However, the Protestant denominations have found themselves so fragmented and divided; one can only wonder where the truth and the Way are to be found. All 41,000 plus denominations that call themselves Christian cannot be just different roads leading to the same place.

Over eighty percent of Protestant Christianity is liberal-progressive as to their biblical and social beliefs, which began in earnest in the late 18th century up until the present. This covers too much area for a summary, but to mention just a few, they treat the Bible as being from man, not inspired and fully inerrant. They prefer to explain away the Bible accounts of miracles as myths, legends, or folk tales. They do not believe in the historicity of Bible characters such as Adam and Job. They say that Moses did not write the first five books of the Bible but that they were written by several authors from the tenth to the fifth centuries B.C.E., and were compiled after that. They say Isaiah did not author the book bearing his name in the early eighth century B.C.E. However, two or three authors penned it, centuries later.

In addition, they claim that Daniel did not pen his book in the sixth century B.C.E., but rather it was written in the second-century B.C.E. They claim that the Bible is full of errors, mistakes, and contradictions regarding history, science, and geography. They claim that the Antichrist is merely good versus evil and is not to be taken literally. Higher criticism has opened Pandora's Box to an overflow of pseudo-scholarly works whose result has been to weaken, challenge and destabilize people's assurance in the trustworthiness of the Bible. Who needs enemies like agnostics and atheists when we have liberal Bible scholars? We have not even delved into their unbiblical views of social justice, gay marriage, homosexual priests, women in the pulpits and far more.

Some may ask what about the remaining twenty percent of Christian denominations. Most of those are moderate in beliefs, which cast doubt on the trustworthiness of the Scriptures and give fodder to the liberal-progressive denominations. These are fence-riders, who have abandoned the Truth and the Way of true, pure worship within Christianity. Before delving into the so-called conservative parts of Christianity, let us look at the charismatics.

We have charismatic Christianity, the fastest-growing segment, which emphasizes the work of the Holy Spirit, spiritual gifts, and modern-day miracles, speaking in tongues[175] and miraculous healing, even snake handling in some areas. All of this is **un**biblical and based on emotionalism.

Those who believe that charismatic Christianity is false Christianity, such as this author, are overly critical. Supporters of Charismatic Christianity say we "should be focusing on the fact that while many in the church continue to abandon our Christian faith, the Pentecostal/Charismatic community continues to offer the church a legitimate growth mechanism."[176]

I would respond that a denomination founded on, grounded in **un**biblical beliefs is not true Christianity, and are the false teachers and prophets that Jesus and the New Testament writers warned us were coming in the last days.

Therefore, charismatic Christianity is no Christianity at all, and all who are being brought in, are being obscured from finding the path of true Christianity. Further Catholicism brought in almost the whole world from 500 to 1500 C.E. Based on the same false, illogical reasoning from above, this would supposedly be a sign of their being true Christianity.

So-called conservative Christianity is so small that it barely receives any press. In fact, most of the press that conservative Christianity does receive, it is attacked from liberalism and atheism. Honestly, we should not confuse radical Christianity, such as the Westboro Baptist Church,[177] with truly conservative, fundamentalist Christianity. However, even here within conservative Christianity, we find differences doctrinally, and yes, even in the so-called salvation doctrines.

---

175 http://www.christianpublishers.org/speaking-in-tongues-truth

176 http://tiny.cc/j5d7mx

177 www.godhatesfags.com/

Are all of the 41,000 different varieties of Christianity just different roads leading to the same place? Are all of the various conservative churches the Truth and the Way? The answer is no, as far as this writer is concerned. We need to return to the question that Jesus asked, "When the Son of Man comes, will he find faith on earth?" (Lu 18:8) Jesus would not find faith on earth, not at the level that one might expect, not at present.

## The Antichrist and Politics

As we just saw, much of the antichrist movement is made up of those alienated from God in their gross human imperfection and religion. Well, here we will discover that governments and politicians can be antichrists as well. We begin with the obvious, communist and socialist governments are liberal-progressive both politically and religiously. They seek to displace any hope for God's kingdom and have its citizens place all their hope in human governments. Any government that oppresses Jesus' disciples are, in essence, in opposition to him. If they are persecuting, oppressing, and opposing Christians, they too are antichrists. – Matthew 25:31–46; Acts 9:5

The position of being an antichrist is not limited to communist countries, as it applies to Islamic countries, even **individual politicians** within a democratic constitutional monarchy (UK, Canada, Australia), and, yes, the federal republic of the United States. This would also apply to the United Nations, which is no friend to Christianity. Many view the United Nations as the world's only true hope for peace and security, which, hope alone, belongs to Jesus Christ. – 1 Thessalonians 5:3

This author is a great advocate of the United States of America, which has served as the protector and police officer of the world. If it were not for the United States, many evil empires, e.g., German, Russian or Islam, would be ruling the world, and we would be living in far worse times.

**Romans 13:1-3** Updated American Standard Version (UASV)

**13** Let every soul[178] be in subjection to the governing authorities. For there is no authority except by God, and those that exist have been placed[179] by God. [2]Therefore the one setting himself against authority has taken a stand against the ordinance of God; and those who have taken a stand against it will receive judgment against themselves. [3] For rulers are not a cause of fear,

---

[178] Or *person*

[179] Or *established, instituted*

not to the good deed, but to the bad. Do you want to be free of fear of the authority? Keep doing good, and you will have praise from it;

The United States has played a very large role in this manner. It has protected the world from evil and has relieved the pains of many. If genocide is taking place, it is the United States' first to respond. If a country is invaded, it is the United States first on the scene. If there is a natural disaster, it is the United States first on the scene. Notice the words of Paul,

**1 Timothy 2:1-3** Updated American Standard Version (UASV)

**2** First of all, then, I urge that entreaties and prayers, petitions and thanksgivings, be made on behalf of all men, [2] for kings and all who are in high positions, that we may lead a peaceful and quiet life, godly and dignified in every way. [3] This is good, and it is acceptable in the sight of God our Savior,

Yes, we are even to pray for political leaders and governments. Why? Paul gives us the answer quite plainly, "that we may lead a peaceful and quiet life." We pray that the government will not enact any laws that will infringe on our religious freedoms, and even that they will even enact some that will expand our religious freedoms. If we can pray for such, why can we not act on behalf of our prayers by voting for the conservative politician over against the liberal one, because he or she is likely to be of the same mind? This is, of course, a conscience decision that each Christian must make for themselves.

However, we do not want to go beyond Scripture. We do not wish to see the United States as the entity that will be used to bring in true peace and security because it is not. Only Jesus Christ and his kingdom will do so. Further, we do not want to see the United States as an arm of God's kingdom; it is not an extension of God's kingdom. In the eight years of the Obama presidency and now the first year of the Biden Presidency, we have noticed that the country has swung liberal-progressive and has failed in its role as the protector and police officer to the world. This should wake us up to the fact that it is nothing more than a human government, ran by imperfect humans, and within a moment, it can be converted into just the opposite of why we had appreciated it. This is not to say that we cannot vote for persons who may get the United States back to its former greatness.

## The Antichrist Uncovered

Jesus was quite clear as to how the world would treat Christians,

**Matthew 24:9-11** Updated American Standard Version (UASV)

9 "Then they will deliver you up to tribulation, and will kill you, and you will be hated by all nations because of my name. 10 And then many will fall away,[180] will betray[181] one another, and will hate one another. 11 And many false prophets will arise and will lead many astray.

Christians are hated because of Jesus' name, which makes any such ones antichrists, "against" Christ. Some of these false prophets were actually former Christians. However, these Christians John says, "went out from us, but they were not of us; for if they had been of us, they would have continued with us." –1 John 2:18, 19.

As we have seen from the beginning of this publication, there is no one antichrist, but many individuals from the time of Jesus first coming in the first century, up unto his return in the future. Being that some of these antichrists are also false prophets, they are in the business of deceiving true Christians. How do they go about this business of deceiving?

## The Antichrist and False Teachings

As we have learned apostasy is standing off from the truth, and any engaging in such are antichrists. The apostle Paul warned Timothy,

**2 Timothy 2:15-18** Updated American Standard Version (UASV)

15 Do your best to present yourself to God as one approved, a workman who does not need to be ashamed, rightly handling[182] the word of truth. 16 But avoid empty speeches that violate what is holy, for they will lead to more and more ungodliness, 17 and their word will spread like gangrene; Hymenaeus and Philetus are among them. 18 men who have gone astray from the truth saying that the resurrection has already taken place, and they upset the faith of some.

On these verses, Knute Larson writes,

> **2:15.** Timothy, by contrast, must do his best to **present [himself] to God as one approved, a workman who does not**

[180] Lit *be caused to stumble*

[181] Or *hand over*

[182] Or *accurately handling* the word of truth; *correctly teaching* the word of truth

**need to be ashamed.** Timothy, and all who follow Christ, are to consecrate themselves to God, working diligently for his approval. The teacher whom God approves has no need of shame in his presence.

God bestows his approval on the one who exhibits truth, love, and godliness in daily living, and who **correctly handles the word of truth.** The false teachers were mishandling God's words, using them for their own benefit. Timothy was commissioned to handle the words of God correctly. All preaching should present the truth clearly, cutting through erroneous ideas or inaccurate opinions.

The pastor or teacher must acquaint himself thoroughly with Scripture. He should familiarize himself with historical information and the context of the passage, especially when trying to reach back through the centuries to gain an accurate understanding of God's revelation.

**2:16.** Paul again issued a warning: **Avoid godless chatter.** Paul was not referring to backyard chats or little conversation groups that met over tea. The phrase "godless chatter" describes the empty babbling of false teachers. Their doctrines may have been quite organized and intricate, but Paul labeled them "chatter" because they were without substance.

In addition, their teachings did not promote the life and practices which God approves. Paul declared that those who indulged in such chatter would **become more and more ungodly**. In vivid contrast to God's truth, which results in godliness, the false teachings degenerate into greater ungodliness.

**2:17–18.** But these false teachers and their philosophies were not pitiful little people to be ignored. They were causing great harm to those whom they influenced: **Their teaching will spread like gangrene.** Just as the teaching they followed was rotten, so its foul and corrupt nature infected more aid more people. In contrast, truth is always life producing, creating wholeness and health. Paul gave two examples of leaders who abandoned the faith and whose spurious teachings brought destructive results: **Hymenaeus and Philetus, who have wandered away from the truth**.

Other than this mention by Paul, these two men pass unknown in history. But because their names were known to Timothy, they were probably leaders within the Ephesian church.

> Yet, they wandered away. This describes a slow drifting from the truth. These men did not make a dramatic break from the Christian faith and run after strange philosophies. They slowly shifted their thinking, toyed with new ideas, held to what they liked and discarded what was unappealing. After a time, they had denied the faith.
>
> Paul highlighted one main point of their false teaching: **they say that the resurrection has already taken place**. This supposition, rampant among the false teachers, taught that the fullness of salvation had come. Consequently, there was no future bodily resurrection, for the true resurrection was spiritual. This led to the practice of discounting anything connected with physical life making daily obligations and concerns for holy living irrelevant. Spiritualizing the resurrection diminished the sacrifice of Christ, removed the necessity of enduring hardship, and promoted immoral living. In this way, **they destroy the faith of some**. (Larson 2000, 287)

Deceptively, Hymenaeus and Philetus taught that the resurrection had already come, and it was merely a symbolic one, meaning that Christians had only been resurrected in a spiritual sense. This is somewhat true on two fronts: (1) When one becomes a Christian, he moves over from death to life (John 5:24; 1 John 3:14), and (2) it is the Christian God made alive even though he was dead in trespasses and sins. (1 Pet 4:3-6; Eph. 2:1-5, See ASV) In these verses, what is meant? Christians were once dead spiritually, but after accepting Christ and having forsaken the practice of sin, they have passed over from death to life in that the condemnation to death that all humans face is lifted, and they have the hope of eternal life. Nevertheless, what Hymenaeus and Philetus taught went beyond this truth, into their denying Jesus' promise of a literal resurrection of the dead under the kingdom of God. – John 5:28-29.

Less than one hundred years after Hymenaeus and Philetus, we have a group called the Gnostics,[183] who developed the idea of a purely symbolic resurrection. They believed that one could acquire knowledge Greek, *gnosis*) in a mystical way. Gnostics fused biblical truths with Greek philosophy and Oriental mysticism. For example, they taught that all physical matter was evil, which would mean that Jesus did not come in the flesh; otherwise, he would have been evil. Thus, they claimed that it only appeared as though Jesus came in the flesh. In other words, it only seemed as though he had a human body,

---

[183] Gnosticism was an early Christian religious movement teaching that salvation comes by learning esoteric spiritual truths that free humanity from the material world, believed in this movement to be evil.

which is known as Docetism, an early heresy that claimed that Jesus Christ was not a real person. As we have repeatedly shown, in the above, this is one of the most direct signs that the apostle John warned against, which made one who professed such an antichrist. – 1 John 4:2-3; 2 John 7.

## The Antichrist Rejects God's Kingdom

The antichrist has another issue, and it is with Jesus' role as the king of God's kingdom, which will rule over the earth. (Dan. 2:44-45; 7:13-14; Rev. 5:10; 11:15) There are some who do not take this literally any more than they take the Antichrist literally. For some, the kingdom is in the mind or heart.—Luke 17:21, See KJV, ASV, and TEV[184]

*The Catholic Encyclopedia* (1910) said under "Kingdom of God":

> The 'kingdom' means not so much a goal to be attained or a place . . . **it is rather a tone <u>of mind</u>** (Luke, xviii,20-21), it stands for an influence which must permeate **<u>men's minds</u>** if they would be one with Him and attain to His ideals.[185]

The Southern Baptist Convention of 1925 put it this way:

> The Kingdom of God is **the reign of God in the heart and life** of the individual in every human relationship, and in every form and institution of organized human society. The chief means for promoting the Kingdom of God on earth are preaching the gospel of Christ, and teaching the principles of righteousness contained therein. The Kingdom of God will be complete when every thought and will of man shall be brought into captivity to the will of Christ. And it is the duty of all Christ's people to pray and labor continually that his Kingdom may come and his will be done on earth as it is done in heaven.[186]

The Southern Baptist Convention of 1963 and 2000 put it this way:

> The Kingdom of God includes both His general sovereignty over the universe and His particular kingship over men who willfully acknowledge Him as King. Particularly the Kingdom is the realm of salvation into which men enter by trustful, childlike

---

[184] A poor rendering, "the kingdom of God is within you," should rather be rendered, "the kingdom of God is in your midst." See NASB, ESV, RSV, HCSB, and LEB The context is Jesus speaking to the unrighteous Pharisees (vs 20), so he would not be saying the Kingdom was in them, but rather that because the king himself was talking to them, it was in their midst.

[185] http://www.catholic.com/encyclopedia/kingdom-of-god

[186] http://www.sbc.net/bfm2000/bfmcomparison.asp

commitment to Jesus Christ. Christians ought to pray and to labor that the Kingdom may come and God's will be done on earth. The full consummation of the Kingdom awaits the return of Jesus Christ and the end of this age.

What does Jesus and the Bible say about the kingdom of God? Jesus said, "My kingdom is not of this world."[187] (John 18:36) Jesus also said, "The ruler of this world [Satan] is coming. He has no claim on me" (John 14:30) Indeed, Paul tells us, at present, "The god of this world [Satan] has blinded the minds of the unbelievers." (2 Cor. 4:4) Now, we can appreciate why Jesus will be removing all present-day governments, becoming the sole ruler over the earth. (Ps. 2:2, 6-9; Rev. 19:11-21) When Christians recite the Lord's Prayer, this is what they are actually praying for, "Thy kingdom come. Thy will be done in earth." – Matthew 6:10, KJV.

Should the kingdom of God be viewed as a real government? Isaiah 9:6-7 says, "For to us a child is born, to us, a son is given; and the government shall be upon his shoulder, and his name shall be called Wonderful Counselor, Mighty God, Everlasting Father, Prince of Peace. Of the increase of his government and of peace, there will be no end …" (ASV, RSV, ESV, NASB, and HCSB) It does have a king, Jesus Christ. (Dan 7:13-14; Mark 14:61-62) Jesus will have co-rulers under him, and they will rule over the earth. (Rev 5:9-10; 20:4; 22:5; Matt 19:28) The word "government" means "a group of people who have the power to make and enforce laws for a country or area." Well, will not Jesus and his co-rulers have power and authority (Matt 28:18), to enforce the will and purposes of the Father over the earth? Whether one sees it as a government or a kingdom, these are synonymous with its purpose.

### The Antichrist Misleads

The Antichrist not only misleads Christians into rejecting biblical truths as to doctrine but also in the case of morality as well. Paul warned, "For the time is coming when people will not endure sound teaching, but having

---

[187] 18:36 **My kingdom is not of this world.** By this phrase, Jesus meant that His kingdom is not connected to earthly political and national entities, nor does it have its origin in the evil world system that is in rebellion against God. If His kingdom was of this world, He would have fought. The kingships of this world preserve themselves by fighting with force. Messiah's kingdom does not originate in the efforts of man but with the Son of Man forcefully and decisively conquering sin in the lives of His people and, some day, conquering the evil world system at His Second Coming when He establishes the earthly form of His kingdom. His kingdom was no threat to the national identity of Israel or the political and military identity of Rome. It exists in the spiritual dimension until the end of the age (Rev. 11:15). MacArthur, John (2005-05-09). *The MacArthur Bible Commentary* (Kindle Locations 48413-48415). Thomas Nelson. Kindle Edition.

itching ears they will accumulate for themselves teachers to suit their own passions."[188] (2 Tim. 4:3) To the Corinthians, Paul writes,

**2 Corinthians 11:13-15** Updated American Standard Version (UASV)

13 For such men are **false** apostles, **deceitful** workers, **disguising themselves** as apostles of Christ. 14 And no wonder, for even Satan disguises himself as an angel of light. 15 Therefore it is not a great thing if his servants also disguise themselves as servants of righteousness, **whose end will be according to their deeds**.

Peter writes,

**2 Peter 2:1-3** Updated American Standard Version (UASV)

**2** But false prophets also arose among the people, just as there will also be false teachers among you, who will secretly introduce destructive heresies, even denying the Master who bought them, bringing swift destruction upon themselves. 2 Many will follow their acts of shameless conduct,[189] and because of them the way of the truth will be spoken of abusively; 3 and in their greed they will exploit you with false words; their judgment from long ago is not idle, and their destruction is not asleep.

He also went on to write,

**2 Peter 2:12-14** Updated American Standard Version (UASV)

Daring, self-willed, they do not tremble when they revile glorious ones,[190] 11 whereas angels who are greater in might and power do not bring a reviling judgment against them before the Lord. 12 But these, like unreasoning animals, born as creatures of instinct to be captured and destroyed, blaspheming about matters of which they are ignorant, in their destruction will also be destroyed, 13 suffering wrong as the wage for their wrongdoing. They count it pleasure to revel in the daytime. They are blots and blemishes, reveling in their deceptions, while they feast with you. 14 having eyes[191] full of

---

188 Professing Christians and nominal believers in the church follow their own desires and flock to preachers who offer them God's blessings apart from His forgiveness, and His salvation apart from their repentance. They have an itch to be entertained by teachings that will produce pleasant sensations and leave them with good feelings about themselves. Their goal is that men preach "according to their own desires." Under those conditions, people will dictate what men preach, rather than God dictating it by His Word. MacArthur, John (2005-05-09). *The MacArthur Bible Commentary* (Kindle Locations 60857-60860). Thomas Nelson. Kindle Edition.

189 Or *their sensuality*; *their licentious ways*; *their brazen conduct*

190 Or *angelic majesties*

191 **Eye**: (Heb. *ʿǎ·yin*; Gr. *ophthalmos*) Both the Hebrew and the Greek can refer to the organ of sight. (Matt. 9:29; 20:34) Illustratively, the eye is an important way of communicating with the mind, which influences our emotion and actions. When Satan tempted Eve, he motivated her through what she saw with her eyes. Eve had seen this tree many times now "it was a delight to the eyes." (Gen 3:6) Satan also tempted Jesus with the things seen by the eyes. (Lu 4:5-7) The apostle John spoke of "the lust of the eyes"

adultery that never cease from sin, enticing unstable souls, having a heart trained in greed, accursed children;

False religious leaders, antichrists, abandon Bible principles,

**Leviticus 18:22** Updated American Standard Version (UASV)

22 You shall not lie with a male as you lie down with a woman; it is an abomination.

**Romans 1:26-27** Updated American Standard Version (UASV)

26 For this reason God gave them over to degrading passions; for their
women exchanged natural relations[192] for those that are contrary to
nature, 27 and the men likewise gave up natural relations with women and
were violently inflamed in their lust toward one another, males with males committing the shameless deed, and receiving in themselves the due penalty for their error.

**1 Corinthians 6:9-10** Updated American Standard Version (UASV)

9 Or do you not know that the unrighteous will not inherit the kingdom of God? Do not be deceived; neither fornicators, nor idolaters, nor adulterers, nor men of passive homosexual acts, nor men of active
homosexual acts,[193] 10 nor thieves, nor greedy persons, nor drunkards, nor
revilers, nor swindlers, will inherit the kingdom of God.

**Hebrews 13:4** Updated American Standard Version (UASV)

4 Let marriage be honorable among all, and let the marriage bed be without defilement, for God will judge sexually immoral people[194] and adulterers.

**Jude 1:7** Updated American Standard Version (UASV)

7 just as Sodom and Gomorrah and the cities around them, since they in the same way as these indulged in gross sexual immorality and having gone after other flesh,[195] are exhibited as an example in undergoing the punishment of eternal fire.

---

as being "from the world."(1 John 2:16-17) The Bible uses the "eyes" to express emotions, like "haughty eyes" (Pro. 6:17), "alluring eyes" (Pro. 6:25) "eyes full of adultery" (2 Pet. 2:14), "whose eye is evil [a selfish man]" (Pro. 23:6) or "an evil eye [a greedy man]" (Pro. 28:22). It can also refer to understanding.–Lu 19:42; Eph. 1:18.

[192] Or *natural sexual relations*; Lit *natural use*

[193] The two Greek terms refer to passive men partners and active men partners in consensual homosexual acts

[194] **Sexual Immorality**: (Heb. *zanah*; Gr. *porneia*) A general term for immoral sexual acts of any kind: such as adultery, prostitution, sexual relations between people not married to each other, homosexuality, and bestiality.–Num. 25:1; Deut. 22:21; Matt. 5:32; 1 Cor. 5:1

[195] Gr *sarkos heteras*; Lit *went after different or other flesh*; i.e., pursued unnatural fleshly desires

**Christians Must Exercise Discernment**

Based on all that we have covered in this publication, it is best that we heed the advice of the apostle John, the one who tells us of the Antichrist. He writes, "My dear friends, do not believe all who claim to have the Spirit but test them to find out if the spirit they have comes from God. For many false prophets have gone out everywhere."—1 John 4:1, GNT

We should follow the example set by the Bereans,

**Acts 17:10-11** Updated American Standard Version (UASV)

10 The brothers immediately sent Paul and Silas away by night to Berea,
and when they arrived they went into the Jewish synagogue.11 Now these Jews
were more noble than those in Thessalonica; they received the word with all eagerness, **examining the Scriptures daily to see if these things were so**.

We pray with Paul,

**Philippians 1:9** Updated American Standard Version (UASV)

9 And it is my prayer that your love may abound more and more, with knowledge and all discernment,

It is as Jesus said,

**John 8:32** Updated American Standard Version (UASV)

32 and you will know the truth, and the truth will set you free."

**What the Bible Really Says About the Antichrist**

**1 John 2:18** Updated American Standard Version (UASV)

18 Little children, it is the last hour; and just as you heard that antichrist is coming, even now **many antichrists** have arisen; whereby we know that it is the last hour.

**1 John 2:22** Updated American Standard Version (UASV)

22 Who is the liar but the one who denies that Jesus is the Christ? This is the antichrist, even the one who **denies the Father and the Son**.

**1 John 4:3** Updated American Standard Version (UASV)

3 and every spirit that **does not confess Jesus** is not from God; this is the spirit of the antichrist,[196] of which you have heard that it is coming, and now it is in the world already.

---

[196] **Antichrist**: (Gr. *antichristos*) The term "Antichrist," occurs in the NT five times. From those five times, we gather this entity is "against" (i.e. denies Christ) or "instead of" (i.e., false Christs) Jesus Christ. There are *many antichrists* that began back in the apostle John's day and will continue up unto Jesus' second coming. (1 John 2:18) The antichrist is referred to as a number of individuals taken together, i.e., collectively. (2 John 1;7) Persons who deny Jesus Christ are the antichrist. (1 John 2:22) All who deny the

**2 John 1:7** Updated American Standard Version (UASV)

[7] For many **deceivers** have gone out into the world, even those who **do not confess the coming of Jesus Christ in the flesh**. This is the **deceiver** and the antichrist.

**A Deceiver Who Deceives**

Lastly, simply know that the antichrist is anyone, group or organization that denies the Father and the Son, Jesus came in the flesh, who oppose Jesus or his kingdom, and his disciples. Also, it is any that deny God's Word as being inspired and fully inerrant, waters down biblical truths, to appease man. It is any that claim they alone speak for Christ, are his representation here on earth, or that they are Christ.

divinity of Jesus Christ as the One and Only Son of God is the antichrist. (1 John 2:22; John 10:36; Lu 9:35) Some antichrists are apostates, one who left the faith and are now in opposition to the truth. (1 John 2:18-19) Those who oppose the true followers of Jesus are the antichrist. (John 15:20-21) Individuals or nations that oppose Jesus or try to supplant his kingly authority are antichrists.–Ps. 2:2; Matt. 24:24; Rev. 17:3, 12-14; 19:11-21.

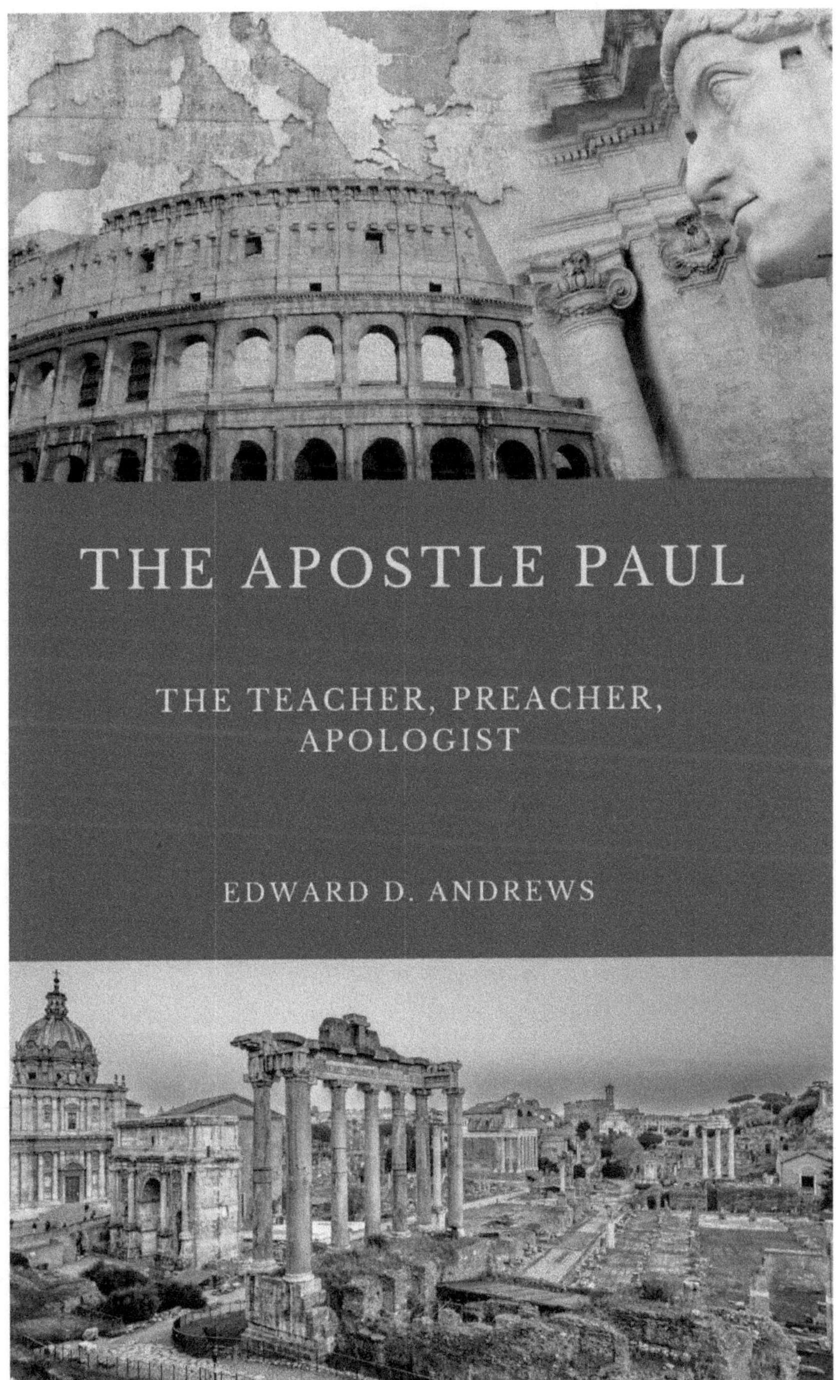
THE APOSTLE PAUL
THE TEACHER, PREACHER, APOLOGIST
EDWARD D. ANDREWS

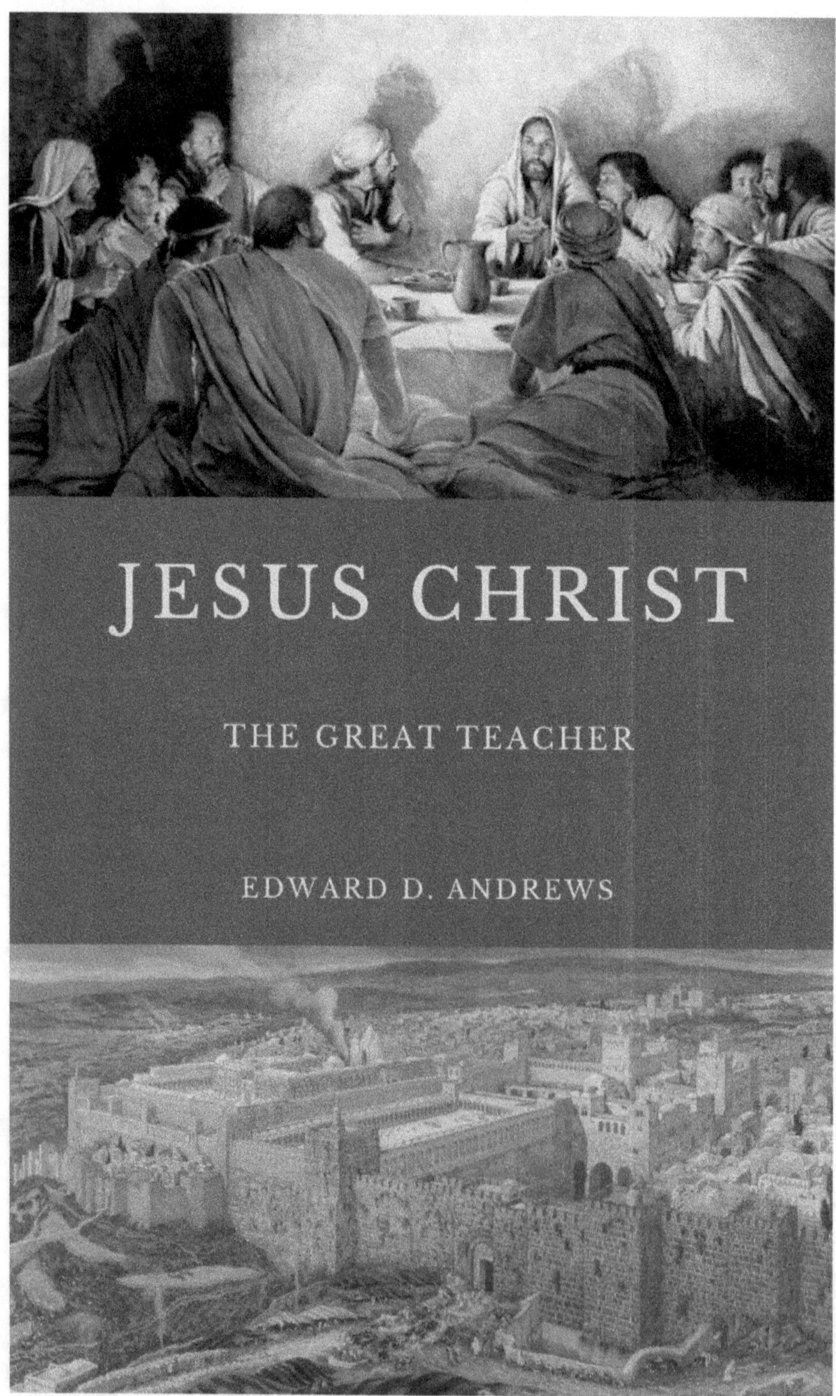
JESUS CHRIST
THE GREAT TEACHER
EDWARD D. ANDREWS

# Bibliography

Archer, Gleason L. *A Survey of Old Testament Introduction. Revised and expanded ed.* Chicago: Moody, 2007.

—. *The Expositor's Bible Commentary, Vol. 7: Daniel and the Minor Prophets.* Grand Rapids: Zondervan, 1985.

Arnold, Clinton E. *Zondervan Illustrated Bible Backgrounds Commentary: Matthew, Mark, Luke, vol. 1.* Grand Rapids, MI: Zondervan, 2002.

Arthur, Alexander. *A Critical Commentary on the Book of Daniel.* Edinburgh: Norman MacLeod, 1893.

Auberlen, Carl August. *The Prophecies of Daniel and the Revelations of St. John.* Edinburgh: T. & T. Clark, 1857.

Auchincloss, William Stuart. *The Book of Daniel Unlocked.* New York: Van Nostrand, 1905.

Barker, Kenneth L., and Waylon Bailey. *The New American Commentary: vol. 20, Micah, Nahum, Habakkuk, Zephaniah.* Nashville, TN: Broadman & Holman Publishers, 2001.

Barnes, Albert. *Daniel. Vol. 2. Notes on the Old Testament. Ed. Robert Few.* Grand Rapids: Baker, 1950.

Bauer, Walter. *A Greek-English Lexicon of the New Testament. William F. Arndt, Theodore Danker, and F. Wilbur Gingrich, trans. and rev., 3rd ed.* Chicago: University of Chicago Press, 2000.

Benware, Paul. *Understanding End Times Prophecy.* Chicago: Moody, 2006.

Black, Allen, and Mark C Black. *THE COLLEGE PRESS NIV COMMENTARY 1 & 2 PETER.* Joplin: College Press Publishing Company, 1998.

Blomberg, Craig. *The New American Commentary: Matthew.* Nashville, TN: Broadman & Holman Publishers, 1992.

Brand, Chad, Charles Draper, and England Archie. *Holman Illustrated Bible Dictionary: Revised, Updated and Expanded.* Nashville, TN: Holman, 2003.

Buter, Trent C. *Holman New Testament Commentary: Luke.* Nashville, TN: Broadman & Holman Publishers, 2000.

Campbell, Donald K., and Jeffrey L. gen. eds. Townsend. *A Case for Premillennialism.* Chicago: Moody, 1992.

Chouinard, Larry. *Matthew, The College Press NIV Commentary.* (Joplin, MO: College Press, 1997.

Easley, Kendell H. *Revelation, vol. 12, Holman New Testament Commentary.* Nashville, TN:: Broadman & Holman Publishers, 1998.

Elliott, Charles. *Delineation Of Roman Catholicism: Drawn From The Authentic And Acknowledged Standards Of the Church Of Rome, Volume II.* New York: George Lane, 1941.

Elwell, Walter A. *Baker Encyclopedia of the Bible.* Grand Rapids: Baker Book House, 1988.

Gangel, Kenneth, and Max Anders. *Daniel, vol. 18, Holman Old Testament Commentary.* Nashville, TN: Broadman & Holman Publishers, 2002.

Goldingay, John E. *Word Biblical Commentary Vol. 30, Daniel* . Nashville, TN: Thomas Nelson Inc, 1989.

Kistemaker, Simon J., and William Hendriksen. *Exposition of the Book of Revelation, vol. 20, New Testament Commentary.* Grand Rapids: Baker Book House, 1953–2001.

Larson, Knute. *Holman New Testament Commentary, vol. 9, I & II Thessalonians, I & II Timothy, Titus, Philemon.* Nashville, TN: Broadman & Holman Publishers, 2000.

Longman III, Tremper. *The NIV Application Commentary : Daniel.* Grand Rapids: Zondervan Publishing House, 1999.

MacArthur, John. *Because the Time Is Near.* Chicago: Moody, 2007.

—. *The MacArthur New Testament Commentary: Revelation 1–11.* Chicago: Moody, 1999.

—. *The MacArthur New Testament Commentary: Revelation 12-22.* Chicago: Moody, 2000.

Mangano, Mark. *Esther & Daniel, The College Press NIV Commentary (: , 2001).* Joplin, MO: College Press Pub., 2001.

Miller, Stephen R. *Daniel, vol. 18, The New American Commentary.* Nashville:: Broadman & Holman Publishers, 1994.

Montgomery, James A. *A Critical and Exegetical Commentary on the Book of Daniel (International Critical Commentary Series).* Edinburgh: Bloomsbury T & T Clark, 1926.

Morris, Leon. *The Gospel According to Matthew, The Pillar New Testament Commentary.* Grand Rapids, MI(; Leicester, England: W.B. Eerdmans; Inter-Varsity Press,, 1992.

Pentecost, J. Dwight, and ed. J. F. Walvoord and R. B. Zuck. *"Daniel," in The Bible Knowledge Commentary: An Exposition of the Scriptures, vol. 1.* Wheaton, IL: Victor Books, 1985.

Ryrie, Charles C. *Basic Theology.* Chicago: Moody, 1999.

—. *Revelation. rev ed.* Chicago: Moody, 1996.

Smith, J. B. *A Revelation of Jesus Christ.* Scottdale, PA: Herald, 1961.

Stein, Robert H. *A Basic Guide to Interpreting the Bible: Playing by the Rules.* Grand Rapids: Baker Books, 1994.

Terry, Milton S. *Biblical Hermeneutics: A Treatise on the Interpretation of the Old and New Testaments.* Grand Rapids: Zondervan, 1883.

Thomas, Robert L. *Revelation 8-22: An Exegetical Commentary.* Chicago: Moody Publishers, 1995.

Vine, W E. *Vine's Expository Dictionary of Old and New Testament Words.* Nashville: Thomas Nelson, 1996.

Walton, John H. *Zondervan Illustrated Bible Backgrounds Commentary (Old Testament): Isaiah, Jeremiah, Lamentations, Ezekiel, Daniel, vol. 4.* Grand Rapids, MI: Zondervan, 2009.

Walvoord, John. *Daniel (The John Walvoord Prophecy Commentaries)* . Chicago: Moody Publishers, 2012.

Weatherly, Jon A. *THE COLLEGE PRESS NIV COMMENTARY: 1 & 2 Thessalonians.* Joplin: College Press Publishing Company, 1996.

Weber, Stuart K. *Holman New Testament Commentary, vol. 1, Matthew.* Nashville, TN: Broadman & Holman Publishers, 2000.

Wilcock, Michael. *The Message of Revelation, The Bible Speaks Today, ed. John R. W. Stott.* Downer Groves, ILL.: InterVarsity, 1975.

Wood, Leon J., R. Laird Harris, Gleason L. Archer Jr., and Bruce K. Waltke. *Theological Wordbook of the Old Testament.* Chicago: Chicago: Moody Press, 199.

Zuck, Roy B. *Basic Bible Interpretation: A Prafctical Guide to Discovering Biblical Truth.* Colorado Springs: David C. Cook, 1991.

www.ingramcontent.com/pod-product-compliance
Lightning Source LLC
Chambersburg PA
CBHW072347090426
42741CB00012B/2958

* 9 7 8 1 9 4 9 5 8 6 6 2 6 *